TOXIC MINDS

HOW TO DEAL WITH DIFFICULT PEOPLE, DISARM NARCISSISTS, AND HANDLE NEGATIVE PERSONALITIES

CHASE HILL

CONTENTS

INTRODUCTION

A few years ago, I found myself in a situation that should have been simple. A friend—let's call him "Kyle"—needed a place to crash for a few days. You've heard this story before: someone's apartment plans fall through, their life gets a little chaotic, and before you know it, your couch becomes their new home.

You'd think it would be easy to tell someone like Kyle to leave, but it wasn't a hostile takeover. Kyle had mastered the art of the low-maintenance guest. He was so good at it that I started to feel guilty. He'd contribute just enough—a dish cleaned here, a grocery run there—that kicking him out felt like evicting someone for being too tidy.

But somewhere along the way, I realized my life was orbiting around his. My couch? His now. TV? Kyle's pick. Even my alone time had to be penciled in between his needs. I had slowly turned into a side character in my own apartment.

Why didn't I say anything? Because I had convinced myself that I was being a good guy. If I spoke up, it would mean confronting the fact that this friendship was less a mutual support system and more like a free Airbnb booking with no checkout date.

I told myself it was just Kyle being Kyle, but really, it was me avoiding conflict. I kept saying, "It's fine," even when it wasn't.

Now, that's the trick with toxicity, right? It doesn't always show up with flashing lights and sirens. It sometimes wears a friendly face, holds a shopping bag full of your favorite snacks, and leaves you too confused to ask, "Why is this draining me?"

But before I continue the saga of my freeloading friend, let me tell you about Jenny.

Jenny didn't notice what was happening until it was too late, and her entire life had been turned upside down. At first, her partner just seemed overly invested in her time. Sweet, right? But then, like an overnight guest who quietly extended their stay, his behavior started to escalate. Plans with friends started getting canceled not because Jenny wanted to, but because her partner "just couldn't handle it" if she left the house. And so, the gradual isolation began.

Jenny thought she was doing the right thing by reassuring him. She didn't want to rock the boat—who does? But by the time she realized how much control he'd taken, she felt completely adrift. Her world had shrunk to revolve around his moods, his needs, and his crises. She had gone from "partner" to "emotional concierge"—responsible for maintaining the fragile balance of his happiness at the expense of her own.

Sophie's story was different. Her toxic encounter wasn't in her personal life—it was at work. She was in the minority at work, so she tolerated more than she should have, fearing that if she spoke up, it might cost her job. Her toxic coworker didn't flip out on day one; it started with "harmless jokes" and slowly escalated into outright racist and sexist comments. Each time Sophie tried to stand up for herself, she was dismissed as "too sensitive." Like Jenny, Sophie found herself stuck in a toxic dynamic that made her second-guess every response.

Like me and Kyle, as well as Jenny and her partner, Sophie had to reckon with a hard truth: toxic people don't often come charging into our lives with obvious malice. They come in quietly, take root, and make us feel like *we're* the ones overreacting for wanting to regain control.

It's the knock-on effect that so many of us have to cope with. It's as if we are being walked all over, but there's nothing we can do about it. You may have noticed this yourself when you try to explain how their actions hurt you, but the conversation takes a turn, and it ends up being your fault. This leaves you feeling powerless, desperate for change that seems impossible to achieve.

It's the isolation that can hurt just as much. Being stripped of your power wrecks your self-esteem, and you naturally lose the strength to enjoy the aspects of life you once loved. As much as you want to talk to someone about the toxicity in your relationship, saying the words out loud can make you feel foolish.

The common thread here isn't that we're all victims of some grand, malicious conspiracy. It's that most of us, at one point or another, have been *too nice*, too accommodating, too willing to put our needs last in the name of avoiding conflict. Whether it's Kyle's indefinite stay on my couch, Jenny's gradual isolation by her partner, or Sophie's daily dose of workplace microaggressions, toxic situations have a way of convincing us that we're stuck.

The truth is, we're not. We've just been tricked into thinking that asking for what we need—space, respect, boundaries—is somehow selfish. But trust me, it's not selfish to want your couch back.

It seems obvious what you need to do, but it's never that simple. You often hear the question, "Why do you keep them in your life?" but you can't find an answer. Deep down, you hope they will change, but there's a constant fear that this will never happen. After so long, you've accepted that this is just how your life is—or worse, that this is what you deserve.

I never wanted to use the word "toxic" to describe some of the people in my life. It sounded too harsh, even cruel. I pushed through my teenage years into adulthood and found myself making excuses for the behavior of others: they were going through a rough time or had suffered in the past. But I believed it wasn't their fault, and I just needed to be more understanding and helpful.

Does this sound familiar? Before you know it, you have lost who you really are. You have changed in order to make the lives of others better, but in the process, you have lost a massive part of yourself. Even to the point where you look in the mirror and can't identify with the reflection.

Unfortunately, toxic people seem to pop up everywhere—at work, in the supermarket, online, and even in our families. When you hear the word "toxic," you might assume that a toxic relationship is one that is physically abusive, and this lack of understanding can lead to normalizing what is happening in your relationship and preventing the crucial change you need.

In reality, toxicity comes with its own spectrum. While physical abuse is no doubt high up on that spectrum, emotional abuse can't be ignored. This could be direct insults, silent treatment, threats, or manipulation techniques. If you are constantly confused by a person's behavior, you don't feel comfortable around them, or you feel bad about yourself when you are around them, you are experiencing the more subtle signs of toxicity.

A toxic person is anyone whose behavior negatively impacts you or your life. They contribute to your stress levels but won't take responsibility for this, and it's highly unlikely you will get an apology from them. A little bit of drama in your life is okay, but when these people turn everything into a song and dance, it's just draining. Even minor cases of toxicity, like not having your needs met, can spiral into long-term issues for you. Despite what you have been told, you are worthy of kind and loving relationships.

Most people see the problems in their relationships and assume it's the other person who needs to change. On the surface, they aren't wrong, but it's probable that toxic people don't see themselves as the problem and are, therefore, unlikely to make efforts to improve. This means that the change is down to you.

To do this, we have to start at the very beginning. This involves looking at ourselves and the paths we took to get to where we are today. **We all have toxic traits that we can bring to a relationship**, just like we all have a past that can hinder the way we view things. Even passivity—letting things slide—can be toxic.

It's this self-reflection and self-discovery that lay the foundation for your strength and confidence. With these two qualities, we can dive into the understanding of manipulation, emotional abuse, narcissism, and sociopathy. Each step of the way, we will cover in-depth techniques to overcome the toxic behaviors you are experiencing so that you can heal and lead a full life where you are in control.

I had to learn the hard way that I had too many toxic people in my life. Growing up, toxic relationships were the norm, so it made sense that most of mine were, too. I became a pushover at work, saying yes to everyone, hoping for an easier time—but it only made things worse.

My breaking point came when I stopped taking care of myself: drinking too much, not exercising, and gaining weight. I hit rock bottom. The only way out was to change. I educated myself, spent a decade studying human psychology, and put strategies into practice. I am a firm believer that knowledge is power, and I created this book with the hope that sharing what I have learned will empower you.

Before we begin this journey, there's one thing you should bear in mind. Everyone has their own story to tell, and because of this, nobody, regardless of their personal or professional experience, has the right to tell you what to do. Whether you choose to remain in a relationship, romantic or not, is a decision only you can make, and it's one you have control over. The guidance you are about to embark on can help you make that decision. While change is never easy, it's far more achievable when you know you have someone in your corner supporting you all the way, someone who has been through that transformation and discovered what meaningful relationships really feel like.

With just one step at a time, you can do the same. You can break free from toxic behaviors and connect with people on a deeper level. You can experience the joy of trust, balance, honest communication, and knowing exactly where you stand in a relationship. Ready to take the first step?

CHAPTER 1: DIFFICULTY: THE ONLY CONSISTENCY

 The only thing more exhausting than being with a toxic person is pretending they're not toxic.

— *GERMANY KENT*

Toxic people are everywhere, like Wi-Fi signals—constantly present, often invisible, and occasionally disrupting your entire day. We've all come across the emotional saboteurs, the ones who remind you they "just want what's best for you" while setting your self-esteem on fire with the gentlest of matches. Being around these people isn't just bad for your health; it's like binge-eating an entire pizza—terrible for your long-term emotional digestion, but it's hard to resist in the moment.

At the other extreme are toxic individuals who can be abusive or manipulative in more harmful ways. For example, think of a controlling partner or a bully at work—people who use fear or intimidation to get what they want. These individuals create an environment of fear and anxiety. And let's not forget the toxic people shaping the broader world. From corrupt politicians to criminal masterminds, they remind us that toxicity isn't confined to our personal lives. It's everywhere—on the news, in the office, even in the grocery store line, making it difficult to avoid its influence.

So, what causes people to be toxic? Some believe it's in their nature, while others point to neurological and behavioral complexities, along with the influence of the environment. Before we fall into the trap of labeling people as good or evil, it's important to understand more about human psychology. This isn't to excuse their behavior, but understanding what makes them tick might just help you figure out why *you keep* getting stuck listening to their life story for the 437th time.

The Tangled Web of Human Psychology

We know that the brain is an impressive organ. We often only refer to it when talking about our intelligence, yet we know it's responsible for controlling every organ and system in our bodies. The human brain has approximately 100 billion neurons and around 0.15 quadrillion connections between them (Choi, 2016). These connections are vital for the exchange of chemicals. These chemicals are known as neurotransmitters, and 100 different ones have been identified. To put it into perspective, it's like imagining the world's busiest traffic and multiplying it by a billion!

Some neurotransmitters are more well-known, like serotonin and oxytocin, often called the "happy chemicals" or "happy hormones." Dopamine, another important chemical, affects our sleep, mood, and impulses and serves as our "reward" system. Gamma-aminobutyric acid (GABA) helps improve mood and reduce anxiety.

When these chemicals are out of balance, they can lead to unhealthy emotions or mental disorders. For example, studies have shown that serotonin deficiencies can lead to increased violent or impulsive behaviors (Society for Neuroscience, 2007). Chemical imbalances can be influenced by what we consume—not just drugs or alcohol, but also the food we eat. For instance, cocaine causes a buildup of dopamine, and junk food can have a similar, though milder, effect. The pleasure we get from a favorite slice of pizza activates the brain's reward system, producing more dopamine.

Despite their nicknames, no single chemical is responsible for feelings like love, hate, or anger. Many chemicals work together, adjusting our mood depending on the situation. When you face danger, for example, your brain produces chemicals that give you adrenaline to help you react quickly. While we can't directly control these processes, medications like antidepressants can help manage mood by altering brain chemistry.

Neurochemicals are just one factor in human behavior. Individual personalities also play a big role. A study from the University of Carlos III de Madrid examined 541 volunteers in social dilemmas and found that 90% fit into one of four personality types: optimistic, pessimistic, trusting, and envious. Interestingly, envy was the most common type, and this "green-eyed monster" can lead people to act in ways that range from difficult to toxic.

Behavior is another factor in human psychology and the way we interact with others. Our behavior is made up of three components: our actions, cognition, and emotions. For example, the weekend is here and you remember that you have to do the shopping (cognition), so you write the list and do the shopping (action), and finally, you feel somewhat stressed and exhausted (the emotions). This is obviously a very simplified example.

All of us are born with neurochemicals and a personality type, but the behavior is learned. We are products of our environment. We learn a lot of our behavior from our parents, which affects how we act in different situations and treat others. Furthermore, our actual physical environment can influence our behavior and motivations. Noisy environments can cause stress, dark rooms bring about a heavy or depressing feeling. Human interaction is improved in environments that feel safe and secure.

So, really, there are a plethora of reasons why people in your life can be difficult. It could just be that they are simply nasty and enjoy seeing you suffer, or there might be underlying conditions behind their behavior.

The Puzzle of Human Emotions

How is it possible that two people can be watching the same movie, yet one finds it hilarious while the other is mildly amused?

Emergency responders face danger every day, while others are too scared to drive a car or fly in a plane. When you look at neurochemicals, personality, behavior, and environments, you start to see how people interpret situations and other people's emotions in different ways. Let's take a deeper look at some examples.

One of the best examples on a global scale is how people reacted to COVID-19. This threat to our health caused a wide range of emotions and actions. Some people went into panic mode, stocking up on toilet paper and disinfectants. Others thought it was all just a conspiracy theory, while many fell somewhere in between.

How people handle stress varies. Some people thrive on it, leaving things to the last minute to feel that rush of achievement. Others find that if they have an overwhelming amount to do, they become even more stressed at the idea of what they have to do before they even start. Then there are those who give up right away, knowing they will never get it all done.

How we view the task ahead dictates how we handle the stress. And it's not only about the things we have to do. We can react differently to financial stress, the stress of arguments in a relationship, or the stress from work.

It's great to see people who take major life changes in their stride. Moving to a new house should be exciting since you are starting a new chapter in your life. Some people make it look so easy, with everything packed and labeled like a military operation. Others are emotionally drained, feeling sad about leaving their home behind.

We can see the same when people have babies and become new parents. Some moms seem to take it all in their stride like it's second nature. On the other hand, due to the chemical and hormonal changes, other women suffer from postpartum depression. Parenting, in general, can be a highly emotional experience, and each person finds their own way to face the challenges. Many parents seek help and advice from others, while others prefer to handle their problems and emotions internally.

It's interesting to see how different people deal with anger directed at them. Do you respond with anger, or are you the type of person who can stay calm? Some people simply laugh, while others become emotional and cry.

When someone we love passes away, we can work through our stages of grief, but it's also common for people to get stuck in a particular stage, unable to overcome the fury or depression. You may have experienced a loss so great that you turned to addiction of some kind, whether drinking, eating, or exercising—anything to fill the void left by the loss.

The experiences we go through as a child, teenagers, and young adults will also affect our emotions and how we interpret things. In fact, the brain isn't fully developed until the age of 25 (Sapolsky, 2018). Think back to everything that has happened in your life before reaching this age, or if you haven't turned 25 yet, at least up until now. Growing up with parents who are unkind and unloving shows their children what to expect from future relationships. Teenagers who witness their parents' divorce often feel that marriage is unpredictable and unstable (Risch, Jodl, Eccles, 2004).

Narcissistic personality disorder also develops before the brain has fully matured. While its cause could be genetic and/or neurobiological, the environment can play a role.

Parenting styles impact children's experiences. Excessive admiration can lead to an inflated ego and a sense of self-importance. On the contrary, children who have been overly criticized may feel like they fall short of perfection. The narcissist might appear to be full of confidence with a superior attitude, but it is often just a cover for extremely low self-esteem.

What Does All This Mean?

It means we can't be too quick to judge people or label them evil or toxic. Personality types and personality disorders all have root causes. We don't just wake up one day and become a people pleaser, self-absorbed, or sociopathic. It's important to decide if the difficult people in your life are making an effort to improve, just like you are now. They might have accepted the fact that they have a problem, sought professional help, and openly communicated with you to overcome their issues. These individuals can still be difficult and hurt you, but they are trying.

Then there are the people in your life who haven't yet recognized their problem. It's going to be harder with them, but not impossible. When you are well on your way to a better life, you will have the tools and knowledge to show them how their life can improve. You will also have a small handful of people who actually enjoy being the way they are. They will never change because they don't believe it's in their best interest. These individuals will be the most challenging people to deal with, but that's not to say that you have to tolerate their behavior. Instead, navigate life around them despite their presence in your life.

One of our first tasks is to start seeing people for who they really are rather than who we want them to be. We tend to create a set of expectations and beliefs about the people in our lives and this often leads us to know only half of who they really are. This is made worse by our previous experiences.

For example, if you were cheated on in the past, it's tough not to start each new relationship with the assumption that this person may do the same. We must set aside our biases and look at each person for who they really are, without ignoring or excusing them for their words and actions. Making changes in our own lives is what will lead to the best outcomes, not wasting effort trying to change those who don't want to.

Next, imagine life without difficulties. It sounds strange, but it would be a little boring. We need challenges and setbacks in our lives because it's these experiences that allow us to learn and grow. I'm not suggesting we should actively go out of our way to find trouble, but going through tough times can teach us valuable lessons. The person who has lost their job and struggled financially can now appreciate the value of money. The person who has loved and experienced heartbreak now knows more about themselves, their boundaries, and what they don't want in a relationship. Anyone who has had to live with an abusive parent or partner has become stronger as a result.

The Roots of Toxicity: Where It All Begins

Knowing that people aren't born with toxic traits leads to the question, "Where does it come from?" Much like human psychology, it's complex. Not even professionals agree on the answer, and there are no conclusive studies that identify a single source of toxicity. One of the major debates is whether toxic traits come from nature or nurture.

Beginning with nurture, some experts believe it's the environment that contributes to toxic behaviors. Toxic people, especially narcissists, will come across as extremely confident, but this is often a mask for very low self-esteem. They may have suffered from past trauma or grown up in families that exhibit toxic behaviors. Children learn so much from their parents or caregivers, so if they see a particular behavior as normal, they are likely to adopt the same behavior.

Stressful households can also create an environment for toxicity. Imagine a parent who is under severe financial stress, and this converts to anger taken out on the children. They are then full of regret and apologies, only to fly off the handle at their next stressor. This lack of consistency in expressing emotions can lead children to do the same. Similarly, if children grow up without their needs being met, physical or emotional, it could cause problems with understanding needs in adulthood, not being able to recognize or meet their own or others.

At the other end of the scale, there are overprotective and overvaluing parents. These parents may coddle their children, making them feel more special than others. Of course, parents want their children to feel important, but studies have shown taking this to the extreme can lead to adults with grandiose narcissistic traits (van Schie et al., 2020). Pampering and allowing children to believe they are entitled has its consequences, even if it's unintentional.

While it's possible to learn toxic behaviors from parents, it's also possible to inherit them, which is the natural side of the debate. Some of the most negative qualities in toxic people are known as The Dark Triad. These traits include:

• **Narcissism:** Egoism, grandiosity, and lack of empathy.

• **Machiavellianism:** Exploitation and manipulation, disregard of morality, toxic self-interest, and deception.

• **Psychopathy:** Lack of remorse, callousness, lack of impulse control, and antisocial behavior (disregarding social norms). (Cikanavicius, 2018)

Research conducted on twins and families revealed that these three traits—psychopathy, Machiavellianism, and narcissism—are partially genetic (Schermer and Jones, 2020). To add to this dilemma, there is the risk of parents passing on these traits through genes and nurture and poor examples of their own behavior.

This doesn't take into consideration mental health conditions, which can also be both genetic or environmental. Personality disorders, especially the Cluster B types, are closely associated with toxic behaviors (Casabiana, 2021). These personality disorders are characterized by dramatics, emotional issues, and erratic behaviors. Examples include narcissistic personality disorder, antisocial personality disorder, borderline personality disorder, and histrionic personality disorder (the need to be the center of attention all the time).

Other mental health conditions such as bipolar disorder, post-traumatic stress disorder (PTSD), anxiety disorders, and depression can all explain a person's toxic traits. Nevertheless, while it can explain a person's traits, it doesn't excuse or justify them, and it's not your responsibility to try and "fix" them. They need to make the decision to seek help before anything else.

Mental health conditions aren't behind all toxic behaviors. Some people may have a lack of emotional intelligence, the ability to recognize and manage their own emotions, as well as recognize the emotions of others. Their words and actions can cause you a lot of pain, but they don't have the necessary skills to see this.

Other people may be overly negative without having any real reason, which can drain you of your energy and can even affect your outlook on life, putting a damper on things that would otherwise be enjoyable. And, of course, there are some people who are just plain mean because it makes them feel good in the moment. Regardless of their motives, intentions, or lack thereof, you still need to put a stop to it.

The Benefits of Overcoming Toxicity

It can be hard to imagine the positive side of your toxic relationships, but there is a lot to learn. Your gut instincts have been telling you something is wrong for a while now and with good reason. The lesson here is to trust your instincts, and this is helped by being aware of the red flags in a relationship. After the chapters on narcissism, sociopath, and emotional abuse, you will know exactly what you are dealing with early on in new relationships, and you can put a stop to such behaviors sooner. Even if you choose to stay in your current relationship, you still may meet new people who are capable of bringing new waves of toxicity into your life.

For your well-being and the health of your relationships, overcoming toxicity enables you to take care of your needs and stand up for yourself with boundaries. The lessons you learn teach you not to settle because you deserve more.

In the long run, your healing allows for personal growth. Imagine how the toxic people in your life are holding you back right now. It could be the coworker who takes all the credit and advances ahead of you or the partner stopping you from reaching your goals. Each step you take adds to the snowball effect of increased strength and confidence. This doesn't mean complete independence and doing everything alone unless that's what you want. Healthy relationships allow for individual growth at the same time as growing together.

Finally, without change from you, toxic behaviors won't disappear but could get worse. Most relationships start with emotional and physical intimacy, as this is how a toxic person gains power. From there, the emotional abuse starts, with small moments of manipulation that can be twisted into signs of love until the psychological effects become so powerful that a person feels worthless. Once the emotional abuse becomes normalized, the risk of physical abuse can increase. There is nothing beneficial about being at the hands of an abuser. Positivity lies in freeing yourself from it.

To put a positive perspective on toxic people: Everyone we meet has a purpose or a lesson to teach us. Instead of disregarding these experiences, we should embrace them. Learning how to deal with them and not letting their actions affect you as painfully as they have in the past will help you create healthy boundaries, which is the key to happiness.

Putting Chapter 1 into Practice

Take some time to assess the toxic people in your life. How well do you know them, and what are their past experiences? Is there any specific reason or event that could have caused their behavior? Instead of focusing on how they negatively influence your actions, see what positive lessons you can take from these difficult relationships.

CHAPTER 2: SOMETIMES, WE'RE THE PROBLEM

 Knowing your own darkness is the best method for dealing with the darknesses of other people.

— *CARL JUNG*

In the last chapter, we explored why others can be difficult. But let's be honest—assuming that everything is always someone else's fault is a bit naive.

Managing difficult people in your life will be tough if you can't take a step back and acknowledge that you might also play a role. This isn't necessarily good or bad—it just is, and no one is perfect. We all have little quirks, habits, and (yes) toxic tendencies that sometimes add fuel to the fire.

Let's face it—if you think you're immune to being a little toxic, that's probably your first red flag. We've all been guilty of it. Maybe you interrupted someone mid-sentence because your story was *obviously* more interesting. Or maybe you "forgot" to return a phone call to a friend in crisis because you were... watching a three-hour Netflix special on the making of potato chips. We've all been there.

Welcome to the toxic club, where nobody really wants to be, but hey, at least the membership is universal.

Now, let's talk about how we see the world—because perception plays a big role in how we interact with others.

How Perception Impacts Our Relationships and Interactions

Imagine a spicy chicken curry with three different people about to eat it. It's the same curry—the same smell, color, texture, and taste—but each person has a unique experience. One person may find it too spicy, another thinks the chicken is dry, and the third thinks the color is off-putting. The same thing can be said about our perception of reality. Fifty people can attend the same party, but everyone will have a different experience of the same reality.

How we view each experience depends on our expectations, our past experiences, and even the mood we are in at the time. Studies support this differing view of reality. When two football teams played a game, the fans were asked to write down all the fouls committed. It was the supporters of the winning team who thought there were twice as many fouls as what their team had actually committed (Hastorf & Cantril, 1954). Since this study, others have gone on to show the same results: that people aren't objective and can see things in vastly different ways.

The best example of this today can often be seen in the home regarding equality. At some point, most of us have argued about the housework and who is doing their fair share. Despite all the facts, the couple doesn't seem to agree on the fair share.

Good People, Toxic Traits

If you recall our definition of toxicity, it's any type of behavior that causes harm to others. Bearing this in mind, it's practically impossible to go through life without committing a single toxic act. As a teen, you might recall when you were filled with rage and told your parents that you hated them. Even if you didn't feel this way, those words were still hurtful to them. Perhaps you said something to a partner or argued with a neighbor that you now regret. None of these would make you a toxic person.

Let's take a look at a couple of specific examples. David is a perfectionist, and he never saw this as a bad thing. In fact, at work, his team consistently achieved some of the best results and highest productivity. He attributed this to his high expectations for both himself and his team. It wasn't until his partner pointed out that his standards were too high that he felt the need for self-reflection. Only then did David realize that, while his team produced excellent results, they were also highly stressed and often felt like they were walking on eggshells around him.

Emma has three children, an array of pets, and a full-time job. There was always something to do, and to her, the concept of self-care felt toxic. She mistakenly believed it was synonymous with selfishness. On the contrary, Emma's lack of self-care led to toxic behaviors like snapping at her family when she couldn't handle the stress.

David expected too much, but he also celebrated his team's victories. Emma struggled to manage her stress, but at the end of the day, she always made time for stories and bedtime cuddles. Their behaviors were incidents, not the norm, and that's the difference between good yet imperfect people and toxic people. By actively working on their personal development, they can improve their behavior.

Nevertheless, these moments of toxicity can fuel an already toxic relationship. David could encounter a lazy, uncommitted person in the workplace. Without knowing how to effectively motivate them, conflict is soon to arise. Emma's partner might lack empathy, and without the ability to understand Emma's point of view, he may even resort to gaslighting, leaving Emma feeling like she's the problem.

Accountability is crucial. Self-awareness is fundamental. Just as you may not recognize the extent of toxic behaviors in a relationship, you may not be aware of the impact of some of your behaviors. As you work through this chapter, don't feel guilty because a lack of awareness isn't the same as burying your head in the sand and blaming others. However, to be in a better position to survive the toxic people in your life, you need to make sure you are working on your own flaws too—and we all have them!

Toxic, or Just Having a Bad Day? A Self-Assessment

We must examine ourselves and decide which behaviors and habits we can improve. You can look at Chapter 1 and see if anything rings a bell. Everything that applies to the toxic people in your life can also be applied to you. Below is a self-assessment questionnaire that will help you gain insight into potential negative traits of your personality.

1. Do you prefer speaking to listening?

2. Do you enjoy drama in your life?

3. Do you struggle to see other people's points of view?

4. Do you find it easy to tell lies?

5. Do you enjoy gossip?

6. Do you spend a lot of time thinking about the past?

7. When problems arise, do you blame yourself or others?

8. Is it easy for you to apologize when you are wrong?

9. Do you hold grudges, or can you let things go?

10. Is it okay to make fun of others to get a laugh from the crowd?

11. Do you make things personal, especially in arguments?

12. Do you downplay other peoples' achievements?

13. Do you take more than you give?

14. Can you be too critical of others?

15. Have you noticed that people tend to avoid you or disappear from your life without a particular reason?

16. Are you passive-aggressive, or do you use emotional manipulation like the silent treatment?

People generally aren't toxic or nontoxic. There are varying degrees depending on the situation. You aren't looking for a yes or no answer to whether you are toxic. It might be that you enjoy drama and gossip, but you are also capable of apologizing and forgiving others and moving on from the past. This points to a person who can have toxic moments but is generally kind and liked. The problem is that the tendency to gossip can seriously impact the happiness of others, and they might perceive you as toxic because of this behavior.

The Power of Acceptance

Acceptance can be an incredibly powerful tool for both past and present scenarios. Your past has shaped the person you are today. Maybe it was a rough childhood, you dropped out of college, or you started a business that didn't take off.

All of these actions have been significant in your life, but many of us still hold tight to these moments. But how is this helping you right now? Is it healthy for you to keep replaying the negative moments in your life?

For years, I held on to the relationship my parents had. I looked at my own relationship and compared the issues, made excuses, and blamed my past for the problems I was having. What I should have done was simply accept that it was what it was. Of course, it isn't as easy as it sounds, but it's your choice to accept what has happened to you so far and move on from it.

In the present, the constant trickle of changes and unpredictable events can leave our minds in the midst of a storm, debating the right decisions to make, why these things always happen to you, and how you will survive. Or you can decide to accept the challenges that get thrown at you. Learning to accept is like an incredible thunderstorm. Before the storm, the air is thick and heavy. The moment of acceptance is like the rain, washing away all the negativity. Eventually, you are left with a clear sky, making it easier to see the right path forward.

Be careful not to fall to the other extreme. As Dylan Woon explains in his "Power of Acceptance" TED Talk, acceptance isn't about a state of doing nothing. If someone steals your car, you don't accept it and start the search for a new one. You do, however, report it to the police and accept that this is the situation you are in at the moment.

You also need to take everything from an accepted situation and learn from it. Back to the car example: you have reported it, which is all you can do in this situation, and you have learned the valuable lesson of choosing your parking area better, perhaps even paying for secure parking rather than leaving it in the street. Reliving the situation and playing the what-if game will only mentally drain you, as you don't have the power to change it.

Once you are able to do this with other areas of your past, you will soon see your perspective change, and future events that would otherwise have thrown you back into a storm can now be handled with a positive outlook.

As I said, this isn't easy. Over time, we have subconsciously trained our brains to maintain a firm grip on negative experiences rather than accepting them. It's become a habit, and we know how tough it is to break a habit. After a certain amount of repeated behavior, actions move from the decision part of our brain (the prefrontal cortex) to the habit area of our brain (the basal ganglia).

For example, when we are learning to drive, our prefrontal cortex is highly active, but after some time, the actions become second nature. Driving is no longer a learning experience that requires decision-making but instead a habit.

For the most part, this makes life effortless as we don't need to concentrate on some of our daily tasks. But it doesn't help us with our bad habits, such as being unable to accept what has happened. We have to learn how to break this habit loop.

To break habits, we must recognize what we want to do differently. In this case, we have to admit when we are too attached to an event. If you have regrets from your past—let's say you didn't make a career change when you had the opportunity and now you hate your job—you have to spot the stress and negativity you feel when you start thinking about what you should have done. Immediately start thinking about what you have learned from it. You are now aware that when opportunities arise, you should carefully weigh the pros and cons before making a final decision.

What Can You Do About Your Toxic Behavior?

By this point, you have taken a closer look at yourself and can now see what parts of your personality or behavior are either toxic or perhaps fueling the behavior of the toxic people in your life. While you shouldn't blame others for what has happened in your life, you also shouldn't beat yourself up for it either—this goes back to acceptance. What has happened has happened, and now it's time to move forward.

Below are some steps to help you turn any negative aspects into positivity and kindness:

• **Take** what you've learned about yourself **and see** if others can add to your new understanding. It's not always easy to spot our own faults, so constructive feedback from people you love and trust can give you a more complete picture.

• **Don't get defensive when receiving feedback**. Avoid blaming others or making excuses, as that's not the point of the exercise. Instead, take note of what they're telling you so you can work on incorporating those changes.

• **Broaden your relationships.** This may sound unusual, but consider whether your friends share similar age, race, religion, or background. While there's nothing wrong with that, expanding your circle to include people from different backgrounds can teach you more about handling unfamiliar topics. You might meet people with first-hand experience dealing with issues like narcissism or building trust.

• **Make necessary apologies.** If your introspection and feedback reveal actions that deserve an apology, now is the time. It doesn't need to be over-the-top, but your apology should be sincere. Think of it as a fresh start.

Begin to address your negative behaviors one by one. When making changes, it is always best to make small changes that will last rather than too many in one go that won't last. For example, if you used to downplay your partner's achievements, you could surprise them with a celebratory dinner. Or if you have a habit of speaking too much or interrupting, you could use a timer, retraining your brain to become a better communicator.

Shedding the Victim Complex

Before we begin, I want to clarify something important. The word "victim" can evoke strong thoughts and emotions in today's society. By definition, a victim is someone who has been hurt, killed, or has suffered because of someone's actions or beliefs (Collins, n.d.). However, many people who have experienced physical or emotional abuse don't like being labeled as victims, which is completely understandable. This section is definitely not about minimizing what has happened to you, and no form of abuse is ever your fault.

The victim complex or victim mentality is when a person thinks they are constantly the victim of other people's actions and that nothing is their fault, despite evidence to the contrary. What's more, they may even have the attitude that the world is just against them and take everything that happens personally.

Like toxic traits, moments of self-pity are normal, but when feelings of hopelessness and pessimism become perpetual, they can impact all areas of life. Unfortunately, those who have suffered from past trauma are more susceptible to the victim complex because of their negative outlook on life. Regardless of past experiences, it's hard to see past the negativity, and this can lead to the unintentional need to seek validation from others. Consider if any of the following sounds familiar.

• You blame others for what has happened in your life.

• The glass tends to be half empty.

• When someone tries to offer you advice, you discount it.

• When someone tries to offer you advice, you feel attacked.

• It's hard to make changes in your life.

• You feel powerless against the problems in your life.

• You hold grudges and find it hard to forgive.

• You see the world as unfair.

• You keep scores in relationships.

Another thing that has to be clarified is the genuine victim complex because of past experiences and those who use the victim mentality as a form of manipulation. Toxic people can cleverly use this mentality of "Poor me" to gain sympathy and attention while avoiding all accountability.

To overcome the victim complex, taking responsibility for your own life is necessary. It requires processing your past experiences, and even getting professional help. This will help you put the past behind you and recognize that the circumstances you have had to deal with so far don't determine where you are going. One great way to start taking control of your own life is to start saying no to the things you don't want to do or don't agree with. This is the first step to being accountable for your actions and not blaming others.

The victim complex may stem from unhealthy coping mechanisms. To help get past this, now is the time to start practicing self-care and prioritizing your physical and mental well-being for healthier coping techniques. Doing so gives you the opportunity to take control of your life and reduce those feelings of helplessness. Self-love can help you see you are worthy of more and have the power to make this happen.

For many, this will seem like an odd chapter for a book aimed at helping you deal with others who are toxic. It's more likely that you aren't toxic and that there are just a few things that you can tweak to make your interactions more fruitful and less confrontational. The key takeaway from this chapter is that nobody is perfect and perspective can help you not just now but also in future relationships. You can only hold yourself accountable for your own behavior—the actions of others are their own responsibility.

Putting Chapter 2 into Practice

Spend some time thinking about potential toxic behavior you may have shown in the last few weeks. Try to put yourself in other people's shoes, even those who have toxic traits. Notice if any particular triggers cause your behavior.

Commit to a week of self-reflection, especially when it comes to conflicts. Consider using a journal to further gain perspective and the role you may play in them. Decide on healthy coping strategies to prevent the behaviors you don't like. After a week, reflect again on the positive changes you have made and continue working on them.

CHAPTER 3: CHANGE STARTS WITH YOU

 If you accept the expectations of others, especially the negative ones, then you never will change the outcome.

— *MICHAEL JORDAN*

There's nothing more empowering than realizing you have the ability to turn a bad situation around. At the same time, the cliché says to "take a long, hard look in the mirror," which can feel almost impossible when toxic people have drained your self-esteem. Instead of feeling empowered, you might only focus on your flaws and feel even worse about yourself.

The point is that if you can get past the words and actions of others, you will be able to look in the mirror and see your true worth. At first glance, you might notice a few extra wrinkles or a stray gray hair, but if you go beyond that and take a moment to really look at your reflection, you'll start to see kind eyes that hold wisdom and kindness to offer—in the right way and to the right people.

Let's go back to those wrinkles we see in the mirror, and if there aren't wrinkles, there could be bags, blemishes, or other signs of a life filled with struggles. The first time I tried this, I made every excuse possible. The bags under my eyes were due to the stress my relationships were causing me. My bad skin was because of exhaustion, which was also due to the stress caused by my relationships. And you can guess why a double chin had appeared! Well, I didn't have the energy to exercise because of the same issues.

What is actually worse than blaming others for your problems is that you are handing over immense amounts of power. If a person has so much control over your life and can cause such negative effects, then they have too much power. It all starts with finding your own power—not a false power, not one driven by your ego or the need to control, but true power.

What Is True Power and Where Does It Come From?

True power is a cocktail of ingredients, including love, the ability to know who you truly are, and the acceptance that we have spoken about before. It's about building your own life in a way that doesn't force things on others, but at the same time, it doesn't mean allowing people to walk all over you. By setting the right boundaries that don't harm you or others, you get to experience an amazing power from within.

For some, it takes a near-death experience to appreciate the power they have, while others start to find it while on a spiritual or religious path. For the rest of us, it starts by learning who we really are. We have already begun this step by looking at our potential flaws and negative behaviors, but there is more to it than that. If you have been surrounded by toxic people for too long, you may have lost touch with yourself.

Take a moment to think about your positive qualities: your big heart and the love you have to give. What things do you like doing? Do you have any hobbies, or have they been forgotten? The same can be said about your goals. What motivates you, and what do you want to achieve in the next week, month, six months, or year? Once you have answered those questions, you can follow some simple steps to finding your true power.

Enjoy the silence. Have you ever noticed that there is constantly some form of noise or distraction in our lives? Your mobile phone is tempting you, the TV is blaring, or someone is always talking to you. It can be draining. Learn to step away from these distractions and appreciate the calming effect of silence.

Start small—turn your phone on Do Not Disturb for an hour, let your email notifications pile up, and accept the discomfort. It's not the end of the world if you don't respond to a meme in the group chat within 30 seconds.

One trick I've found useful is turning ordinary, mindless tasks into intentional, quiet moments. Whether it's brewing your morning coffee or taking a stroll around the block, put your phone away and just let your mind wander. You won't believe how much quieter everything becomes when you stop multitasking.

Follow a routine. A routine is an excellent way to establish control over your life. It also allows you to structure your day to be efficient and save time. While every routine should allow for some flexibility, organizing your daily tasks into a routine allows you to focus on the more challenging aspects of each day.

Spend more time with those who make you feel positive. We will discuss this further later, but first, you need to create more free time by saying no to those who create negativity. Surrounding yourself with positive energy gives you strength.

Take care of your body. You don't have to go on a super strict diet or head to the gym every day. Regular exercise, such as walking, swimming, or even activities like yoga, is perfect for the body and the mind. Getting more exercise will help you sleep better, and when you combine this with a balanced diet, your energy will increase.

Create a happy home. Again, in terms of your relationships, we will look at this more later on, but there are other ways to make a happy home. It always helps if your home is tidy and, of course, comfortable. When you get home at the end of the day, you need a safe haven where you can relax.

Meditate. Meditation is an extremely valuable tool to connect with your inner power. Not everybody finds it easy to meditate, at least not in the beginning. It helps you focus, calm the mind, and reduce stress and anxiety. You will find that this **guided meditation** video for inner strength and power will help.

Scan the QR code above to open the meditation.

All of these steps will guide you toward discovering yourself and your true power. Only once you appreciate the power within you can you effectively apply the rest of the advice in this book. So, how do we go from finding our power to experiencing freedom?

Turning Your Power into Freedom

While not blaming society, I've come to realize that in our society, it's not easy to express our true feelings. People ask how we are, and we respond with "fine," "good," and "okay," even though we aren't. If we discuss our problems, we're considered a negative bore, and if we talk about our successes, we are simply showing off.

Even when we find our power, there's still a weight burdening us. We have to realize that the only way to get rid of this weight and allow the power to work its magic is by speaking our truth.

There's no need for you to continue suffering in silence. The traumas we experience are too much to struggle with alone. By sharing these experiences, you help yourself and others. Imagine living with an abusive partner. You meet up with a friend who has recently lost their job and their home, and you tell them everything is fine.

Alternatively, imagine if you told your story and opened up about the pain you have experienced. The chances are that other people will also feel more confident about telling their stories and releasing their own burdens. We have seen this on a global scale with movements such as Black Lives Matter or Me Too.

By speaking the truth about our situations, we understand that we aren't alone and that there is a strong community of people who are going through similar experiences. This is empowering for all involved.

Confiding in just one person will enable you to create a much deeper relationship with that person — a genuine friendship built on honesty instead of what we think we should say. What's more, speaking the truth opens the door to new perspectives you hadn't thought of. Your friend might have words of wisdom regarding your abusive relationship, and they will also be able to highlight your positive qualities and, most importantly, remind you of your self-worth.

It's not always easy to open up and share your feelings, especially when you fear being laughed at, told to get over it, or having your experiences belittled. Not everyone has someone in their life to whom they feel comfortable talking. In this case, therapy can be a great solution. Even then, I know that the idea of speaking to a complete stranger can be more terrifying than talking to a friend.

If you're not quite ready to share your truths with the world, at least try keeping a journal. This will be an effective way to start opening up and lessening your burden while you continue to find your inner strength.

Remember that there is a difference between sharing our difficulties and traumas and just complaining all the time. Whether it's your journal or your friend, speaking the truth is about freeing yourself from what prevents you from becoming stronger.

Complaining about the weather, the traffic, and your partner at every opportunity isn't productive. If you start venting, your friend might join in, and then both of you will end up feeling drained. To ensure that both of you walk away feeling lighter, relieved, and more connected, it's better to focus on the more significant, deeper troubles you are going through or have gone through.

Recognizing How Your Choices and Beliefs Limit Who You Are

The choices we made in the past have led us to where we are today, and that's fine because we've accepted it. However, the choices you make from now on will impact every aspect of your life. Each choice we make comes from our thoughts. As we've seen, our views on reality will impact our decisions, but we can't forget about the thoughts and beliefs we create about ourselves. Let's look at two examples:

1. Life is hard. You are stressed, tired, and generally not enjoying yourself. There's a lot of bickering and arguing within your relationships, and you know that a vacation is going to break the cycle and give you a chance to press reset. After a week of rest, you notice that life is definitely better, but it only takes a week, maybe two, for things to start slipping back to how they were.

2. You separated from your partner a while ago and have just started socializing again. At a party, ten people compliment you, but one person makes a comment that offends you. Rather than let your confidence shine for once, you obsess about the one negative comment.

Both of these scenarios go back to the same issue: your thoughts. Although you are making an effort to change your situation, you are caught up in changing your environment or circumstances rather than getting to the bottom of the issue, which is your thoughts about life. You can change your environment by taking a vacation, but it only temporarily changes your thoughts. You have done well by leaving a toxic partner, but until you see yourself in a new light, your mind will still be trapped in that relationship.

Your thoughts are at the root of everything. When you think badly about yourself, your self-esteem decreases. You speak quietly and look down at the ground. You don't have the confidence to make the right decisions, so your choices may not always be right.

On the other hand, when you are able to think about yourself in a good way, your body language reflects this. It becomes easier to see past the gray, which means that alternative paths light up. These alternatives enable you to see problems from different angles and make better choices.

The trick is to take our focus away from what we perceive as the problem and recognize that the real issue is our perception of the problem. You may feel ugly, but the problem isn't that you are ugly —the problem is that you think you are ugly.

When we can change our thoughts on a situation, the solution becomes easier. The solution, in this case, isn't that you need to lose weight, change your hairstyle, and buy new clothes. The solution is to change the way you think about yourself.

Self-Limiting Beliefs Tear You Down

A self-limiting belief is any thought we hold onto about ourselves or the world around us that holds us back from achieving all we want to. It's every time you tell yourself that you can't do something or that you don't deserve something. Perhaps it's those times when you convince yourself you're too old, too tired, or not smart enough. Instead of deciding you need to make changes to achieve your goals, you avoid the potential source of pain as a way of protecting yourself from it.

These types of thought patterns often stem from childhood and get reinforced as the years pass. They can be incredibly debilitating because, at the same time as preventing your growth, they are assumptions you have made rather than facts. For example, you may feel powerless in your current situation, but the truth is, you just don't have the right skills yet, which you have the power to change.

Self-limiting beliefs can lead to a self-fulling prophecy. If you tell yourself enough times that you are powerless, you stop standing up for yourself. If you believe your thoughts and opinions aren't worthy of being heard, you stop expressing yourself. The longer you spend not standing up for yourself or not speaking up, the more you reinforce the self-limiting belief. If you are wondering just how powerful these thoughts can be, anywhere from 85 to 95 percent of what we do on a daily basis is based on our subconscious (Barberio, n.d.).

Sadly, holding onto these self-limiting thoughts is quite toxic. They can intensify the idea that you don't have a right to your dreams and goals, professional or personal. It's even likely that you won't begin the healing process because you feel you aren't worthy of a happy life full of positive relationships.

Everyone deserves the right to be able to heal and move on. Without falling back into the victim complex, our pasts can be filled with emotional pain, whether that's from the loss of a loved one, ended relationships, job loss, illness, or abuse. Healing is the process of working through these experiences, unraveling the emotions attached to them, and accepting them. It stops these experiences from intensifying and having even more of an impact on your relationships. As harsh as it might sound, choosing not to heal is choosing the victim mentality. Though it might be painful, what's on the other side is illuminating, refreshing, positive, and empowering, and no limiting belief should get in the way of this.

And for the toxic people in your life? Yes, they also deserve the opportunity to heal. They have suffered their turbulent pasts and hold on to this, perhaps more than we know. They might not be ready to heal; they may even be in complete denial about their need to heal, but they still deserve to lead a happy and fulfilling life. Remember that their past doesn't condone their behavior, and it's not up to you to heal them. You can lead a horse to water, but you can't make it drink. Instead, focus on setting the right example and work on your own self-limiting beliefs and healing.

How to Crush Limiting Beliefs and Take the Wheel

We need to take all of our limiting beliefs and first appreciate that the only thing they are doing is holding us back. They are not a method of self-protection. I often hear things like, "Yes, but if I don't start a new relationship, then I won't get hurt again." It sounds like you are trying to protect yourself, but in reality, you are limiting your chances of finding a loving partner.

Your homework for Chapter 3 is to take some time to understand why you tolerate certain behaviors, how to stop putting up with them, and finally, how to overcome your limiting beliefs. We'll achieve this through the following steps:

1.Determine why you tolerate certain behaviors

Why do we often let others take advantage of us without speaking up? Or if your family insists you do things you don't want to, why is it easier to get angry and walk away rather than establish a firm boundary?

We often tolerate these types of actions because we may have been subjected to control, criticism, excessive praise, neglect, or a combination throughout our childhood. As children, we developed coping methods for these treatments, such as withdrawing, becoming passive and subdued, or becoming angry. We carry these coping methods with us into adulthood.

If you lived with a parent who insisted you did everything their way, you may have tried to fight it as a child and realized your efforts were fruitless. When you find yourself in a controlling adult relationship, you continue with the same behavior you learned as a child. So ask yourself, what behaviors do you tolerate, and where does this come from?

2. Determine the source of your limiting beliefs

Just like you tolerate behavior you don't like, your limiting beliefs also have their origins. Perhaps you were told by a teacher that you would "never get anywhere in life with that attitude," or even something seemingly innocent like, "You need to find yourself a husband/wife." These kinds of comments can make us believe we can only reach our full potential when we are married.

3. Reset your beliefs

Whatever you were told in the past does not reflect your life today. Remember that when you listen to what toxic people tell you, you are handing over your power. Your attitude can be the key to what will drive you forward. You don't need to get married to be complete. It's the complete opposite; you need to be complete before starting any new relationship.

4. Find role models who align with your positive beliefs

To reinforce your new belief, find people who can back up your new thoughts. For example, if you believe that getting married is not necessary for feeling complete, seek out people who live their lives how they want to while still maintaining healthy relationships. Similarly, if you think you're ugly, spend time with those who compliment you and accept their kind words.

5. Imagine the worst-case scenario

Imagining the worst-case scenario isn't the same as living it. Just because you have pictured it doesn't make it destiny. What it does is prepare you for every possibility.

If you're debating a career change, the worst that could happen is that you absolutely hate it. If that's the case, you need to be prepared to search for another job.

On the other hand, to avoid focusing too much on the negative could also involve meeting new people, networking, learning, or advancing up the career ladder. When you consider the worst-case scenario, you'll see that at the end of the day, you'll survive it!

6. Test your new beliefs

Go out with friends and see how many people actually call you ugly. Instead of constantly feeling like you're missing out on something, be confident in being single. Pursue that new job! Did the worst-case scenario happen? In the unlikely event that it did, you're still standing. If the outcome is positive, it's a validation of your new belief. Proving our old beliefs wrong enables us to break free from our outdated perspectives and leads to growth.

7. Go back to the behaviors you tolerate and make small changes.

Now that you have reset your beliefs about yourself, you'll have a new sense of confidence. You'll start to feel like you're worthy of respect and appreciation.

If you go out of your way to cook a nice dinner to make your partner feel loved and special but don't get a kiss or even a thank you, either tell them that their actions have hurt you or stop making the dinners! If you become angry, learn how to calm down. If you prefer to stay silent instead of causing conflict, learn how to communicate effectively. We'll cover this in more detail later on.

I felt completely weighed down by my parents' toxic behavior. Nothing I could do would ever make them happy or proud or elicit any type of reaction. I spent years trying everything to get them to notice me. I told myself over and over again that I was the problem and that I couldn't do anything right for them.

When I finally understood that the problem wasn't me, but that I was trying to change myself to make them happy, I realized I needed to change myself to make myself happy. That was when I broke free from not just one toxic relationship but, soon after, all the negative relationships I found myself in.

It can be challenging to look at yourself in such an honest way and prioritize your beliefs and thoughts ahead of those around you. It's even more difficult to have faith in them. But you can do it. Before moving on, enjoy this time of self-discovery because, ultimately, it's all about you!

Putting Chapter 3 into Practice

Take a piece of paper and draw a circle in the middle. Inside the circle, write down all the things specific to your life and within your control. Outside the circle, write down all the things that are out of your control. Keep this piece of paper in a visible place as a constant reminder of where you should focus your efforts.

CHAPTER 4: SOCIOPATHY 101: UNDERSTANDING SOCIOPATHS

 A sociopath will do anything to win. Anything.

— DENZEL WASHINGTON

Before we take a closer look at sociopathic causes and behaviors, I want to clear up the common misconception between a sociopath and a psychopath. TV and movies throw the terms around quite interchangeably, and clinically, they are somewhat similar.

Sociopaths and psychopaths both have antisocial personality disorder (ASPD). We also hear these words to describe extreme behaviors such as serial killings and mass murder.

While this is possible, many of them are just as likely to be a wolf in sheep's clothing, appearing like any other human being.

Sociopath vs. Psychopath: Spot the Difference

A sociopath is someone who clearly shows that they don't care about the feelings of others. It is extremely difficult for them to form emotional attachments, meaning that work and life at home can be difficult to maintain. Sociopaths are impulsive in their negative behavior, especially when it comes to their temper. That being said, they can recognize their bad behavior but will always have some justification for it.

Psychopaths, on the other hand, are capable of pretending to show that they care—the keyword is pretending. Psychopaths can't form real emotional attachments, so their relationships won't be meaningful or genuine. It's possible for psychopaths to love, but it will be on their own terms. Being in a relationship with a psychopath can be particularly hard because they are cold-hearted and won't recognize the struggles and pain of others. It's common for psychopaths to use a "normal" life to cover up illicit activities.

It's also worth mentioning that both sociopathic and psychopathic behaviors have a spectrum. It's possible for psychopaths to feel emotional pain and want to be loved, but it's their own behavior that makes this difficult (Martens, 2020). Violence is also possible for both, but it's just as likely that they are violent toward themselves as to others.

We include an understanding of both because if you notice either of the tendencies, understanding the differences will enable you to choose the best ways to deal with these toxic people. Always bear in mind that many people have not been diagnosed, so they are unaware of their own disorder.

What Lies Behind a Sociopath

The diagnosis is crucial here. We can't go around saying that everyone who has angry outbursts is a sociopath. Narcissism is a personality disorder that takes selfishness and self-obsession to an extreme, but that doesn't mean they are a sociopath. While you may have suspicions about a sociopathic personality, only professionals can correctly diagnose it.

One dictionary definition of a sociopath is someone "who is completely unable or unwilling to behave in a way that is acceptable to society" (Cambridge Dictionary, 2021). This is rather general, as what is acceptable to society changes rapidly. More specifically, sociopaths lack empathy and will not consider the rights or feelings of others.

Manipulation is their go-to technique, but what can hurt the most is that they will show no guilt for the pain they cause. If you smack your head on a barrier, there will be no empathy, so they won't be able to recognize the pain you feel. If a sociopath pushes your head into a barrier, they won't feel guilty about it.

Now, if you look at all of your relationships, it may seem that many people in your life are now sociopaths. I call this "Doctor Google Syndrome." We get the feeling that we know the diagnosis because of one or two symptoms. When we research this, every internet symptom suddenly relates to our situation.

Keep in mind that we are all capable of detaching ourselves from painful situations, which can lead us to appear sociopathic. When going through a divorce, you can either be left devastated or choose to dust yourself off and continue with life. Hearing about a school shooting will leave most feeling awful for the families involved. However, someone who is anti-guns might make a comment about irresponsible gun laws, which can come across as insensitive and unempathetic. Ultimately, these reactions stem from our personal perspectives and beliefs about the world.

If you notice some of these typical characteristics and behaviors in your relationships, it's best to take the safest and most effective actions so that you can start living your life freely.

Here are some of the red flags that could point to a sociopath in your life (WebMD, 2020):

• A complete lack of empathy

• Impulsive behavior

• Using threats or aggressive behavior to control people

• Using charm or intelligence to manipulate people

• Telling lies for personal gain

• Not learning from their past mistakes

• Struggling to form meaningful relationships

• Violence, stealing, and other crimes

• A lack of responsibility when it comes to their job or responsibilities

• Turning to drugs or alcohol

You also need to remember that sociopaths are exceptionally good at masking their disorder in the real world. A colleague who manipulates others can seem like they are highly career-driven. Those with a demanding job can use this as an excuse for their lack of meaningful relationships. Sociopaths either don't care about the damage their actions cause, or they are unable to recognize it.

For this reason, sociopathy is often undiagnosed and left untreated.

How Does Someone Become a Sociopath?

The classic debate between all psychologists is "nature versus nurture." When we look at the nature of sociopaths, we refer to the genetic and biological factors. Nurture, however, is the environmental influence that leads to certain disorders, both psychological and behavioral.

The nurture debate dates back to 1690 when philosopher and physician John Locke believed that almost all human behavioral traits develop from environmental influences. He coined the term "tabula rasa" or "blank slate" in human developmental psychology. This theory is based on the idea that all babies are born with a blank slate and no built-in mental content.

In the early 20th century, John B. Watson took theories from Freud and developed the origins of behavioral psychology. He went on to be known as the father of purist behaviorism. Watson believed that psychologists should focus on behavior that is observed rather than that of the inner mind.

Watson's most famous quote highlights his idea that cultural influence dominated any heredity contribution:

"Give me a dozen healthy infants, well-formed, and my own specified world to bring them up in, and I'll guarantee to take anyone at random and train him to become any type of specialist I might select—doctor, lawyer, artist, merchant-chief, and yes, even beggar-man and thief, regardless of his talents, penchants, tendencies, abilities, vocations, and race of his ancestors" (Watson, 1930).

Another of the most consequential psychologists of the 20th century agreed with Watson. In a television interview, B.F. Skinner stated, "Give me a child and I can shape him into anything" (Skinner, 1972).

The significance of these works is that all favor nurture over nature. This implies that sociopathy, as with other antisocial personality disorders, is a result of how children are brought up. Maltreatment and abuse are clear examples.

Children who suffer from abusive parents are more inclined to grow up to become aggressive, unempathetic, or struggle to form meaningful relationships.

When looking at nurture, we can also include trauma as a cause of sociopathy. Due to antisocial personality disorders going undiagnosed, studies are difficult. This is why most research has been carried out on those who have committed crimes or violence. After extensive brain mapping, scientists have been able to show a link between trauma to the brain and criminal activity. This is known as acquired sociopathy.

The first case was that of Charles Whitman, a former marine sniper who killed 16 people in one day in 1966. His autopsy revealed a brain tumor. Without being biased, some would argue that Whitman's history as a marine sniper could have been a psychosocial stressor and the cause of his violence rather than the brain tumor.

The first published study came from the University of Glasgow. The report included 239 eligible killers and found that 21.34% of them had had or were suspected of having a head injury (Alley, 2013).

One infamous serial killer in Dr. Clare Allely's report was Fred West, who, along with his wife, killed at least 12 people. West was involved in a motorbike accident at the age of 17, which left him unconscious for two days.

Two years later, he was pushed down the stairs by a woman he was trying to abuse, causing a further head injury.

This is certainly not to say that every person who displays sociopathic tendencies is going to go on to be a serial killer! But this is another factor of nurture, whether from childhood abuse or physical trauma, which can lead to sociopathic behaviors in adult life.

Naturally, there are always two sides to every argument. Some believe that nature is a cause of antisocial personality disorders.

Due to the structure of the brain, some people are simply born this way. When using EEGs and MRIs, scientists are able to see the role of the enzyme MAOA, which regulates the emotions in the amygdala and hippocampus. It causes low levels of impulse control in people with antisocial personality disorders (Journal of Forensic Research, 2014).

Aside from an imbalance in chemicals such as dopamine and serotonin, sociopaths may have an abnormal superior temporal gyrus—the scientific term for the area of the brain responsible for the perception of emotions, comprehension of language, and social cognition. So, those in favor of the nature debate will say that a sociopath has structural damage to the brain that has been present since birth.

Interestingly, while many use the terms sociopath and psychopath interchangeably, experts today now believe that the difference between the two is in how they start getting the symptoms. Both are antisocial personalities, but it is now believed that the behavior of a sociopath is created (nurture) and a psychopath is born with their behaviors (nature).

None of this is supposed to scare you. We have looked at the causes of sociopathic behavior in an attempt to better understand the toxic people in our lives, much like we did in the first chapter. Learning the root causes of people's behavior enables us to see things from their point of view. However, as I have also said and must reiterate, understanding is not the same as excusing or tolerating.

How to Spot a Sociopath Before They Run the Show

After reading the previous section, you might feel that the toxic people in your life are not sociopaths or psychopaths because they aren't running around committing crimes and plotting mass murders. These are extreme examples, and as mentioned, those with antisocial personality disorders (ASPD) are excellent at hiding the behaviors that they don't want you to see.

Because of this ability to mask behaviors, it's more likely you know someone with ASPD. The prevalence of psychopathy varies from study to study. In general, 1% of the population has psychopathic traits, so you only need to know 100 people! According to the *Diagnostic and Statistical Manual of Mental Disorders*, 2013, the prevalence of sociopathy is 4% of the population, or one in 26 people you know would show sociopathic traits.

As we have already mentioned the red flags to help you spot a sociopath, we will now look at specific examples of how people with ASPD may do things.

1. Turn up the charm

There are people in the world who are naturally charming, and it's normal for us to be drawn to these personalities. But their charm is consistent, no matter who their audience is. People with ASPD are able to adapt their charm, so if they're interacting with an introvert, they may dial back their charm, while they might increase their charm when talking to an extrovert.

2. Change your opinion of others

If you meet a new person and at first you like them but then notice characteristics that go against who you are, it's your choice not to like them. If you like someone, but then someone with ASPD starts to gossip or fill your head with poisonous ideas about the other person to make you change your mind, you are witnessing the initial signs of ASPD.

3. Be disloyal

Just as quickly as they convince you not to like someone, they could be this other person's best friend the next day. The lack of empathy and connections with others makes it very easy for them to switch sides in an argument, especially for their own gain.

4. Play the guilt game

Both sociopaths and psychopaths are able to make you feel as if you are to blame for everything. You might try to have a calm conversation about a concern, and all of a sudden, you are the dramatic one; they can't do anything right, and you are constantly complaining. Regardless of how you handle a situation, they will make you feel as if they are the victim. They will also use this as an excuse for not getting along with others because the other person is at fault.

5. Act as though they are above the rules

Despite being highly intelligent and understanding of rules from a game to social interactions, these rules won't apply to them. They have a genuine belief that the same rules you live by don't apply to them. This is certainly the case when it comes to financial gain.

6. Be your most trusted confidant

To manipulate your emotions so they can get what they want, they first have to get you to open up to them. Once they have gained your trust and you start sharing your feelings, they will then have ammunition to use against you. Remember that ASPD is largely about not showing interest in other people's emotions, so question why this person is so keen to help you.

7. Weave a confusing web of lies

People with ASPD will change their stories depending on their audience and their goals. Eventually, so many story changes turn into a complex web of lies that not even they can keep up with. If you spot a lie and present this to them, they will turn the tables. You might feel that you are the paranoid one, and they will have the skills to cause you to doubt yourself.

8. Have a hot and cold personality

On the one hand, they will be very good at controlling their personality. On the other hand, the lack of impulse control and angry outbursts can lead people with ASPD to appear rather Jekyll and Hyde-like.

9. Show no remorse

We all make mistakes at some point, some of which are larger than others. Most people can work through what they have done, appreciate that they are at fault, and feel remorseful. The next natural step is to apologize. ASPD causes them to have no sense of their wrongdoing, or they just don't care. As a result, they won't feel remorseful.

10. Sweep you off your feet

Those first few dates are crucial for laying the foundations of a potential relationship. Some signs are a little too good to be true. The charm is obviously going to attract you to a person, but then watch out for inappropriate attention, such as intense eye contact, showering you with gifts, and any form of physical or verbal attention that you are not comfortable with. You are three times more likely to meet a man with ASPD (National Library of Medicine, 2013), but that is not to say that women aren't just as capable of making you feel like you are instant soulmates.

Sociopaths in Real-Life Scenarios

Christine was excited about the possibility of working for an advertising agency, but the company owner refused to negotiate on the salary. A few months later, the company reached out to Christine again to see if she was still interested. She met with the company owner, who told her he was angry about the negotiations but agreed. At the time, Christine hadn't seen this anger as a red flag.

It was the lies that opened Christine's eyes. Her boss had asked her to lie to clients about her qualifications and the size of their company. The final straw came when the owner of the company had an aggressive outburst toward a highly qualified staff member and then proceeded to fire her for no legal reason. Christine's boss was cold, harsh, deceitful, and impulsive (Day, 2020).

Tom was Charlotte's second husband, but it wasn't until a few years had passed that she became worried about some of his traits. It started with completely reckless spending habits. Then the lies came, and disturbingly, he seemed to find pleasure in other people's suffering.

After some years of unemployment, Tom got a new job that required him to spend a lot of time away, which served as a cover for his cheating. Upon getting caught, Tom asks for forgiveness and even sheds a tear. Naturally, things didn't change, and one day, the other woman phoned Charlotte, revealing that Tom had told her that he was divorced and accused Charlotte of cheating. In response, Charlotte changed the locks, infuriating Tom, and filed for divorce, but he still owes her $12,000 and shows no remorse (Lovefraud Reader, 2023).

Patric knew she was different as early as kindergarten when she noticed she didn't have the same emotions as other children. There was no compassion when a classmate fell and hurt themself or guilt when she lied. As she got older, she turned to crime to fill the sense of nothingness she felt. She described it as claustrophobic, and the more she tried to ignore what was happening, the worse it got.

Patric gained a better understanding of sociopathy, but that wasn't enough to find romantic feelings for her husband or an overwhelming love for her children when they were born (Main, 2024).

Every person's story is unique and valid. And you don't need to have experienced financial hardship or have a mother incapable of showing you any emotions to put a stop to sociopathic behavior.

Putting Chapter 4 into Practice

Use the following checklist to identify and track the sociopathic behaviors of others.

• They know right from wrong but don't care

• They are enchanting just to get close to you, but then things change

• They are dishonest and deceitful

• The worst of them comes out when they don't feel they have control over you

• Easily angered

• Will do whatever it takes for personal gain

• Lack of guilt, remorse, and empathy

• Irresponsible or impulsive behavior

• Disregarding social norms and breaking the law

CHAPTER 5: FIGHTING
THE SOCIOPATH

 Letting go doesn't mean that you don't care about someone anymore. It's just realizing that the only person you really have control over is yourself.

— *DEBORAH REBER*

You can't just switch off your emotions. Your history may not have been all bad, and those fond memories still pull on the heartstrings. What's more, there is a tricky thing called the sunk-cost fallacy, where people stay in unhealthy relationships because of the time and effort they have invested in the relationship. Regardless of your thoughts on the future of your relationship, now has to be the time to protect yourself, which is well within your control.

Self-Protection and Dealing with a Sociopath

First and foremost, if you have a sociopath or psychopath in your life who has a tendency to become violent or you fear for your safety in any way, please get help! Don't tell yourself it's a one-off or they didn't mean it. I know how incredibly hard it is to call the authorities on someone you love but consider looking at it from a different point of view. What if you don't report them, and they take their anger out on someone else?

You are going to feel responsible. What if this isn't the first time, and the next time, they end up putting you in the hospital or worse?If you don't feel comfortable contacting the police, reach out to a friend or relative who can help you.

You should also have a plan in place for when a person does turn violent. A good plan is to have a bag prepared with your essential documents, an extra phone, and a copy of your car key. You can also set up a separate bank account—even if it only has a couple of hundred dollars in it, you know you have enough to leave immediately if needed.

If you don't know anyone to stay with, there is no shame in contacting a shelter for victims of abuse. Your plan will have to be more structured and detailed if children are involved. Whenever possible, leave when the other person is not at home!

Of course, not every situation is going to lead to violence. Here's how to handle a sociopath (and protect yourself in the process):

1. Don't try to fix them

A sociopath may not even be aware of their own behavior and are rarely willing to get the required help. Unfortunately, only qualified psychotherapists can provide specific treatment, so you can't fix them. Trying may only make the situation worse.

2. Avoid disclosing personal information

Because of their need to manipulate, it's always best not to share too much with a sociopath. For example, you shouldn't discuss your salary with an ASPD partner because they can try to use this against you when it comes to paying for things. You should also avoid talking about your other relationships and the details of your work.

3. Trust your instincts

It's perfectly normal to question your instincts if you've had your confidence knocked. Try not to focus on the past and listen to what your gut is telling you now. More often than not, we can sense a lie or manipulation. Have faith in this and try to take a step back instead of reacting and getting wrapped up in their reality.

Never take their words as truth if you feel otherwise; instead, question everything.

4. Set your boundaries and say no

Your boundaries are crucial for your safety and mental and physical well-being. Your boundaries express what you are comfortable with and what you aren't.

For example, you might be happy moving in with someone but don't want to combine your finances. Even when someone insists, you have to remain firm on your no.

This will help to protect you from manipulation.

5. Find the give and take

While there will be some rigid boundaries that are not to be crossed, there are other situations where you might be able to find a solution that doesn't cross your boundary but also stops the sociopath from becoming angry or violent. As with the example before, you might agree on a joint account but still keep your separate accounts.

6. Walk away when necessary

In some cases, it takes all our effort not to get upset or angry. As you are only responsible for your own words and actions, sometimes the best thing you can do is put some space between you and the other person. People with ASPD want to see a reaction, so they keep pushing. Walk away, take some time to process how you are feeling, calm down, and when you are ready, you can go back to the situation.

7. Spend time on other relationships

Make the most of the positive relationships in your life. These could be friends, family, work colleagues, or even someone you just say hi to at the supermarket. You will be able to find strength in your other relationships that will help you when dealing with sociopaths.

8. It's what they do, not what they say

Think about Randall Terry's quote, "Fool me once, shame on you. Fool me twice, shame on me." We have all heard the words, "I will change/I have changed/I'm a different person now." This might be true, but words are easy to say, especially for a sociopath. You will only know if they mean it when you start to see a change in their actions.

9. Talk to a professional

Just because you don't have ASPD, it doesn't mean you aren't under immense pressure. Some people are more comfortable talking to a stranger than to a friend, and a professional counselor will be able to help you understand what you are experiencing and offer guidance.

10. Know when it is best to end the relationship

Ending a relationship or cutting ties with a family member is never going to be easy. It's a personal decision that only you can make. You shouldn't feel guilty about this decision, and you have to be careful not to let them use their manipulative techniques to get you to stay. It's best to cut off all communication with a sociopath when you end a relationship. This means blocking calls and messages and deleting social media profiles. Cutting all contact reduces the chance of them being able to change your mind.

Getting Ahead of Sociopathic Manipulation

Once you start implementing the above points, you'll be able to create some emotional distance between yourself and the relationship. With this space, you can disarm their manipulative behaviors with some relatively simple strategies. Detaching yourself from conversations is also helpful. Avoid allowing yourself to be the subject of the conversation and only say what is absolutely necessary. Stop yourself from using any fluff or filler words like "Um" and "Well," as this could signal to the sociopath in your conversation that you are nervous. Small talk is great for conversation topics because it protects you from deep and meaningful conversations that can then be used against you.

If conversations do get personal, keep your answers short and simple. The other person is expecting you to show your vulnerability, so when this doesn't happen, they can be thrown off their guard. As a sociopath's emotions are limited, it can be hard for them to talk about how they feel, so simple questions to keep in your arsenal are "How are you feeling?" and "How do you feel about…?"

Once you gain a little confidence while communicating with a sociopath, you might be tempted to fight fire with fire. Instead of just allowing them to criticize you, you point out their flaws. I would be very cautious about this for two reasons. Firstly, you would be sinking down to their level, and you are better than that. Secondly, it's more likely that this person just doesn't care about what you think. You may even irritate or anger them. It's best to preserve this energy and use it for techniques that have a greater impact.

Removing a Sociopath from Your Life

You have done well to decide to break away from the sociopathic person in your life, and you have taken that all-important first step. As with any "breakup," it's hard to remain strong and not start thinking about what you might be missing, whether the person has changed, or if you just made a huge mistake.

Your instincts have told you this was the right choice, and we know that sociopaths seldom change. It's far more effective to focus on a brighter future than dwell on a dark past.

Here are some tips and tricks to help you move past this type of toxic relationship:

• Do not contact them! We can't stress this enough. We may be tempted to send a reminder about the AC filters or a happy birthday message. Doing so gives power to the other person; they will see a small crack and work their way back in.

• Don't search for them online, drive past their home, or ask mutual friends about them. Most of the time, we just want to know they are doing okay because that's the nice thing to do. Nevertheless, you are only torturing yourself. You might start to reminisce about the good times and forget or minimize the main reason you left in the first place.

• Lean on friends during tough times. Nobody likes being reminded of the horrible times in a relationship, but if you are finding it particularly hard to stay strong, use your friends to help you through these moments. A good friend won't tell you what you already know, but they'll remind you of why you ended the relationship in the first place.

• Know your triggers. A trigger is anything that can lead you into the same patterns or behaviors as before. Personally, my triggers are birthdays, holidays, and anniversaries. Knowing that these are grim times, I can prepare myself in advance so that I'm better able to resist slipping back.

• Take extra care of yourself. Self-care and patience are two essential factors for recovering your power. Acknowledging that recovery takes time will prevent you from being hard on yourself when things don't bounce back to normal as fast as you had hoped. During this time, you can exercise, focus on your diet, explore new hobbies, make new friends, and relax.

Managing the Emotional Pain of Ending Your Relationship

In some cases, recovering from the emotional pain caused by a sociopath requires self-care, self-compassion, and finding your inner strength to move forward. That doesn't mean to say it's a walk in the park. As you read through the chapters, you will embark on ways to help the gradual process of healing from emotional pain. Here, we will focus specifically on what happens when you struggle to break the bond you have with a sociopath because, as mentioned at the beginning of the chapter, you can't just switch your feelings off.

A trauma bond is a bond that stops people from leaving an abusive relationship, and a lot of this is because of intermittent reinforcement or the cycle of trauma bonding. Stages include:

1. Love bombing

2. Gaining trust

3. Criticism

4. Manipulation

5. Resignation

6. Distress

7. Repetition (Psychology Today, n.d.)

This isn't a weakness on your behalf. It's human nature to form bonds, and it's not something you can or should stop doing. You bonded with the wrong person because you felt genuine love for them. This means you can't blame yourself for the bond you created. Not only is your brain programmed to be loyal to your abuser, but the cycle of trauma reinforces this bond. Unfortunately, you might be stuck in the cycle of trauma bonds from past relationships, and unless you break it, you may find yourself in similar situations in the future.

An effective way to stop blaming yourself is with the defense mechanism called reality training (Darcy, 2023). Write a list of everything this person did. While a journal can be used to process emotions, this list should remain factual and avoid any form of justification for the actions mentioned. Next, take your list and imagine yourself from the perspective of another person, someone who is kind and empathetic, perhaps even the future version of yourself who has successfully broken free from this cycle. This person wouldn't dream of blaming you when reading the list.

Though one part of your healing should be strictly for facts, your emotions can't be ignored. Abuse from a sociopath can cause dumbing of emotions or emotional dysregulation, the rollercoaster of intense emotions. Take several pauses in your day to consider how you are really feeling. Don't allow yourself to say that you are okay when you know you aren't. Also, don't allow yourself to feel guilty for emotions like joy and anticipation. Take this reflection to the next level. If you are sad, ask yourself what the source of this sadness is. If you are frustrated, question the source of this frustration. It's going to hurt, but it's the antiseptic for a wound—it's necessary for healing!

Imagine this moment is your tabula rasa—your blank slate. The hardest part is over, and with the strategies in this chapter, you'll be well on your way to self-empowerment. You'll grow in both strength and confidence and most importantly, you'll be aware of sociopaths and avoid making the same mistakes again. This is refreshing in itself!

There is one area of sociopathy that I have not discussed, and that is narcissistic behavior. This is intentional, as I wanted to focus more on narcissistic behavior in the next chapter.

Putting Chapter 5 into Practice

Picture your life a year from now. How would you love to imagine it, with or without the sociopath in your life? Perhaps you have decided to end the relationship, and you can visualize yourself well on the road to recovery. Or maybe you have broken the cycle of trauma bonding, and you are in a healthier relationship. Visualize this future in detail and often!

Exercise: The "Will This Matter?" Test

Think of the latest drama with the sociopath. Now, ask yourself: Will this matter in a year? If the answer's "no," let it go. Repeat as needed.

CHAPTER 6: NARCISSISM 101: UNDERSTANDING NARCISSISTS

 A narcissist will always have an excuse for their behavior, and it's never their fault.

— *MELANIE TONIA EVANS*

One of the biggest traits of a sociopath is narcissism. It can also be one of the most shocking and painful things that we have to deal with when it comes to toxic people. With antisocial personality disorders, the emotional path is very much up and down.

But here's where it gets tricky: not all narcissists are sociopaths, and vice versa. Although narcissism can be part of a personality disorder, it's not sufficient to make a diagnosis. So, while sociopaths may have some narcissistic traits, not all narcissists are antisocial.

Now, living with a narcissist? That's like trying to win a game you didn't know you were playing—only you're constantly reminded that you'll never be as good as them (or as interesting, or as deserving of that last slice of pizza). Sure, we all have days when our self-esteem needs a little pep talk, but living with someone whose sole purpose seems to be undermining your existence? That's a whole new level of psychological whiplash.

The best solution is to recognize the characteristics of a narcissist and steer clear of them before any type of meaningful relationship is formed.

But if you're already entangled with one, there's hope. You just have to figure out how to handle situations *before* they devolve into the emotional equivalent of a reality TV meltdown.

What Is a Narcissist?

Talking to a friend recently, I noticed that the word "narcissist" is often greatly misunderstood. He was sharing about the pain of his breakup and the distance from his children that he was now facing. His ex had called him a narcissist. I was taken aback because all I could see was a broken man trying to do what was best for his children and even his ex, who is the complete opposite of a narcissist.

This led me to a thought-provoking *Los Angeles Times* article from 2011. Today, we completely overuse and misuse the term narcissist. It's like the go-to insult people use, perhaps because it makes them feel more powerful.

Throughout the 90s, we started to see more emphasis on making yourself happy, putting yourself first, and following your goals. And this truly is a good thing. But the downside is that anyone showing more ambition than the social norm or those with self-esteem were then labeled narcissistic.

While it might be a healthy reminder to keep things in perspective and not to trample over others to achieve our goals, in my friend's case, calling someone a narcissist was a hurtful thing to say. Throwing a word around without understanding its true meaning creates a much deeper problem, and now the word "narcissist" has lost its impact.

To put it another way. Think about your definition of the word "classic." We think of classic groups like the Beatles, Queen, and Abba. Classics are defined by the lengthy period of time that they remain of excellent quality. As soon as the word became slang for "awesome" or "cool," it took away some of the true meaning of classic. The same thing has happened with the word "narcissist."

The origin of the word "narcissism" comes from Greek mythology —Narcissus fell in love with his own reflection in a pool of water. It means chasing the satisfaction of your egoistic admiration (Wikipedia). Today's definition hasn't changed, but it has been expanded on. Narcissistic personality disorder (NPD) is a condition where one sees themselves as having more importance than others —they expect special treatment and for others to see them as better. There is also a lack of empathy, a longing for perfection, and a desire for the best of everything. It may seem that a narcissist has all the confidence in the world, but this is often just a front.

With frail self-esteem, any type of criticism will add to the difficulties you have when dealing with them. Despite appearances, narcissists feel incredibly upset when they don't receive the attention that they feel they deserve. Because of the lack of empathy, they are unable to see how certain things affect you and so can't fathom why they aren't getting their attention. What's more, if they see others receiving praise or attention, they can become envious, leading to anger and even depression.

Although you might not see this side of them, narcissists can feel a lot of insecurity and shame. This, toppled with anger issues, impatience, and frustration, is going to make relationships at home and work problematic.

Like sociopaths, narcissists can't see that they are in the wrong. This makes treatment very difficult as they won't actively seek help—they are above this! Narcissistic personality disorder requires treatment from a psychotherapist.

What Causes Narcissistic Personality Disorder?

The exact cause of NPD, like many personality disorders, still doesn't have a definite cause, and again, can go back to the nature vs. nurture debate. That being said, it is more likely to be a combination of the two factors.

If we look at nature first, studies have suggested that genetics plays a role in NPD. Heritability is a metric used to measure the likelihood of genetic influence on a person rather than environmental influences. There is a moderate to high chance of NPD being heritable ("A Twin Study of Personality Disorders," 2000).

When it comes to the structure of the brain, a smaller hippocampus and amygdala have been linked to antisocial behavior seen in narcissists. This is because of the malfunctions in the way people interpret the information received from their senses. Unlike what we have seen before, NPD hasn't been linked to brain trauma. Instead, the trauma is more likely to be a result of childhood environmental trauma.

Parenting styles are often attributed to NPD, and this isn't limited to parents but to all primary caregivers. NPD can be caused by either extreme parenting style.

A parent can completely withdraw attention, causing emotional detachment. Overindulging or being too permissive or even too strict may also impact the behavior of children in their adult years. Other environmental contributions could be abuse (verbal, physical, and/or sexual) and unrealistic expectations.

More recently, cultural influences have also been shown to add to the likelihood or severity of narcissism. NPD is more prevalent in modern societies compared with those that are more traditional ("Modernity and Narcissistic Personality Disorders," 2014).

Be careful of trying to diagnose people who are under 18 years old with NPD. This is because it is extremely complicated to diagnose a personality disorder when a personality is still developing. Those with teenagers may nod their heads while reading some of the symptoms and start to look toward themselves for blame.

Many teenagers will go through phases that can include narcissistic traits, but this is only a part of their development. If you are concerned about your child, you can still seek professional advice.

Are There Different Types of Narcissism?

Narcissism has its own spectrum, meaning there can be different types and degrees. Bear in mind that there is no official number of types. Some are popular among professionals, and others have been researched. For an overview of narcissistic behavior, we will look into the most common types of narcissists.

1. A healthy narcissist

Everyone has a little bit of narcissism in them. It's good to celebrate our wins and to feel proud of the things we do well. It's also healthy to recognize that you deserve respect and happiness. For an official NPD diagnosis, people need to show a minimum of 55% of the most common traits.

2. The overt narcissist

Many would call this the classic narcissist, the person who is self-obsessed, lacks empathy and believes they are superior to those around them.

They are loud and need to be the center of attention. They have little to no respect for boundaries and will try to gradually break down any boundaries you set.

3. The covert narcissist

A covert narcissist is the opposite of an overt narcissist. This type is also known as vulnerable narcissism due to extreme sensitivity.

They live for praise and take criticism very badly. In addition to being envious of others, they will also claim that their problems and sadness are far greater than those of others.

4. The malignant narcissist

These people are just nasty and can be aggressive or sadistic. They enjoy watching others suffer and are masters of manipulation to witness this pain. The malignant narcissist is tough to deal with because of their intelligence, which is directed into manipulation.

5. The psychopathic narcissist

Though not as common, psychopathic narcissists are aggressive and violent and show no remorse for their actions. Typically, serial killers and mass murderers are psychopathic narcissists.

6. The somatic narcissist

The physical body is of extreme importance to a somatic narcissist. They might have to be the best looking or the fittest, so they focus on their weight and appearance. While this doesn't sound too bad, they will put their needs above all others to achieve their idea of physical perfection.

7. The cerebral narcissist

Cerebral narcissists are intelligent, but that is not what defines them. They feel that their intelligence makes them superior to others and will go out of their way to make others feel stupid. Regardless of whether you are right or not, you will never win a debate with them and will probably just end up doubting your own intellect.

8. The bullying narcissist

The name gives you a clear idea of what a bullying narcissist is. They have to win by any means. They socially mock others, put them down, and generally make people feel bad about themselves. A "normal" bully does this to climb the social ladder, while a bullying narcissist has personal motivations.

9. The sexual narcissist

Sexual narcissists may also show traits of somatic and cerebral narcissism, but this is on top of their self-admiration of their sexual abilities. They need to hear how good they are in bed and are obsessed with their performance. Most of their manipulation is related to sex, and it's not uncommon for them to be unfaithful, time and time again.

10. The love bombing narcissist

Love bombing alone may feel amazing in the beginning. The bombardment of affection, kind words, and unexpected gifts in the early days of a relationship may even seem normal. However, narcissistic love bombing is a manipulative technique used to hook a person into a committed relationship before they become aware that they are being played.

11. The celebrity narcissist

This is also known as acquired situational narcissism (ASN) and is related to the acquisition of wealth or fame. Due to so much attention, some people can start to believe they are more important than they are.

Identifying the Narcissist in Your Life

Now that we have clearly defined what a narcissist is and the different types, you probably have a good idea of whether or not you're dealing with one. Still, there are a few other signs worth being aware of:

• Your initial interactions were amazing, but things quickly turned sour.

• They dominate conversations both in topic and the amount of speaking.

• They fish for compliments to feed their self-worth.

• You never feel like your emotions are heard or cared about.

• They don't have any long-term friendships.

• They are gaslighting you, causing you to doubt everything.

• You never get an apology or see any attempts to compromise.

• If you try to break away, they will panic and then become angry.

• You are constantly being controlled by them.

• They don't take responsibility for their actions.

• Everything is either good or bad.

• They project their negativity onto you—if you don't support them, you are pessimistic, etc.

• Their lack of empathy makes it hard for them to work with others or as part of a team.

One word of advice is not to start imagining things that aren't really there, although it's a habit many of us have. If your partner forgets to pay one bill, it might just be an irresponsible moment. This isn't enough to include on your list. The signs have to be something that is regularly seen. We all have moments in our lives when some of these signs have rung true for us too. You may find that numerous issues are relevant. But if some aren't, there is no need to go searching for problems that aren't there.

The Myths Surrounding Narcissism

Because the media has warped the idea of what narcissism is, it's only natural that there are various misconceptions. A dominant myth is that narcissism is caused by bad mothering. We have covered this one because although parenting styles can contribute to personality traits and disorders, there are other influencing factors.

Another myth is that narcissists are aggressive. The problem with believing this myth is that you may assume that the person in your life isn't a narcissist because they aren't aggressive, and you end up overlooking other behaviors. Aggression is not part of the defining criteria of NPD, but it's true that the more aggressive the person is, the more severe the NPD (Lancer, 2023).

Finally, not all narcissists are aware of their behavior because they have been living in this distorted version of reality, which is pretty much all they are used to. Everything they experience, from their thoughts to their emotions, is normal for them. Pointing out their mistakes or highlighting that they might have a problem is fruitless unless they are ready to make a change. You might be inclined to try and explain your feelings to them, hoping that they will change, but it's unlikely that they will change without self-motivation to do so, even if they do listen.

Narcissists in Real-Life Situations

Martin worked in sales, and although he didn't have an official title, he had been on the team the longest. That was enough for him to see himself as above the rest. During a team meeting, the leader highlighted a mistake that Martin had made. This caused Martin to explode and accuse the leader of personally attacking him when it most certainly wasn't part of his responsibility. As Martin continued to ramble on, he proceeded to take credit for work that other team members had done, and whenever someone went to correct him, he silenced them with a hand in their face. After the meeting, Martin took the time to chat with each team member, reinforcing what he had done and complaining about other team members.

Jessica loved cooking and experimenting with new recipes, and her husband initially thought this was a great quality in her. As time passed, Jessica noticed comments like, "Oh, but you make such a great curry" and "What I need after a day like I've had is your curry." These comments made Jessica feel special until she realized her husband was now controlling everything she ate. Then it moved on to the clothes she wore and the people she spent time with. When she tried to talk to him about this, he would gaslight her with, "You just can't remember that we had X for dinner last week" or "Are you serious? We went out with Y last month; you made the plans." Neither of these was true, but the way he said it made Jessica doubt herself.

Jenny and Katlin had been friends since junior school, but Katlin had never felt that their friendship was balanced. When it was the two of them, Jenny was full of kindness and affection. Jenny felt lucky to have a friend who was always there to offer advice. The older they got, the more the imbalance was felt. Around other friends, Katlin was the butt of all Jenny's jokes, and she felt less and less significant. Advice started to only benefit Jenny, like when she told Katlin to stop dating a guy because she could do better, only for Jenny to start dating him. Even then, Jenny was "just doing Katlin a favor." Jenny didn't just have her confidence shattered—she felt like she was less worthy as a human being.

People trying to deal with a narcissist invest a lot of time and energy into a relationship, hoping that the narcissist will change, so much so that it's only themselves that ends up changing. It's time to redirect that energy toward making positive changes in your own life.

Putting Chapter 6 into Practice

I know you're eager to see changes quickly, but now that you have a more complete understanding of the different types of narcissism and the behaviors they display (intentional or not), take some time to observe the narcissist in your life. You will probably notice many "Ahh, that makes sense now" moments, and more importantly, you will feel reassured that the issues in your relationship aren't all your fault.

Exercise: The "Reality Check" List

Each time the narcissist in your life makes a comment that leaves you questioning yourself—whether they're subtly undermining, guilt-tripping, or bragging—jot it down in a "Reality Check" list. Next to each comment, write a brief "reality check" of your own.

Example:

Their Comment: "You're too sensitive; I was just joking."

Reality Check: "My feelings are valid, and a joke shouldn't make me feel small."

This exercise helps you challenge their narrative and remind yourself of what's real. Over time, your "Reality Check" list will become a tool to steady yourself, keeping their influence in perspective.

CHAPTER 7: OVERCOMING THE NARCISSIST

 You will never get the truth out of a narcissist. The closest you will ever come is a story that either makes them the victim or the hero, but never the villain.

— SHANNON L. ALDER

Picture this: You've just spent an hour listening to a narcissist talk about themselves. Now you're wondering if you even exist anymore. Welcome to toxic person fatigue. Let's get you back to normal.

Here is the mistake I made so many times, not just with one narcissist but with all of them.

Each time I made a commitment to changing my own life, I was only 99% on board. There was always that 1% that kept telling me they would change, which held me back.

That's the reason why Alder's quote was so inspiring for me. I appreciated the straightforwardness, villain or hero. Removing that option for change made it easier for me to get past that niggling tiny percentage that was stopping me from being my priority!

What Can You Do If There Is a Narcissist in Your Life?

We are going to assume that there are certain narcissistic people in your life you can't break free from. We are also going to assume that they don't recognize that they have a problem, so professional help is not going to be an option. The first crucial step when dealing with these people is to focus on your boundaries.

The reason we took the time to observe the narcissist and their behavior is so that you are fully aware of what you are being subjected to. At the same time, you now understand that underneath that grandiosity, there is a very fragile ego. While this still isn't an excuse for their behavior, the knowledge you have now is the foundation for defending yourself.

Much like dealing with a sociopath, you must be emotionally strong to handle a narcissist. Self-care is one way to start gaining your strength, and we will go into more detail on this later on. Another strategy is to start surrounding yourself with a strong support system, whether that's friends, family, or even support groups. These trustworthy people will help you stay grounded and remind you of your reality. Don't forget that narcissists will attempt to isolate you from anyone who disrupts the control they have over you, and they will even go to the extent of influencing the people in your support system. This is where online support can be especially useful as not only do the people in these groups have similar experiences, but they also can't be influenced.

Before you start making any changes, check in with your expectations of your relationship. We are now working on the theory that the narcissist isn't going to change.

Another expectation to manage is the emotional connection to expect. Because of their limited emotional connections, you may find that your relationship will never have the same depth as you would like. Only you can decide if this is something you want or not. To gain inner strength, expect nothing from them and focus on your happiness.

Why Are Boundaries So Important When Dealing with Narcissistic People?

Conversations about how things make you feel are going to fall on deaf ears and just waste your energy. Boundaries remove the need for emotional explanations. They are your rules that everyone must follow, and if they don't, there will be consequences.

To create your boundaries, imagine drawing a large circle around you. Think about all of the situations that you are having difficulties with. Take one situation and decide how close you can get to the line and still feel comfortable. What is the one thing that takes you over the line?

For example, your partner criticizes you in public. You might be okay with this in front of good friends and family, but absolutely not in large social situations or with your work colleagues. You might also feel that you won't tolerate any form of criticism in front of others. Nobody can create boundaries for you; it's a personal thing.

We know full well that a narcissist is going to push your boundaries, regardless of how well you express them. This means it's essential for you to have consequences when they do cross a boundary. Using the same example, you might choose to walk away from the situation as soon as they criticize you. Whatever you decide, you have to be 100% confident that you are going to follow through with it.

Communicating your boundary should be short and simple: "I will no longer tolerate you criticizing me in front of others. The next time it happens, I will leave." And full stop! Don't feel you have to justify your boundary. The best thing is to change the subject so they don't have a chance to manipulate you.

Once you start putting your boundaries and consequences into action, you will notice that certain cycles are broken, and this is a great starting place. You will start to notice your confidence improving as you know you can do this.

Here are some other tips for dealing with a narcissist.

Try not to get caught up in their emotional games.

You'll now be wise to the games they are trying to play and recognize when you're being manipulated. Unfortunately, your reaction will provide more ammunition, and the best thing you can do is take a big step back. The next time you think that the narcissist in your life has only said something to get a reaction from you, just say "Okay." This way, they won't have anything to turn back on you.

Choose your battles wisely.

If the situation calls for it, just say "Okay." However, if you feel that their behavior crosses a line or a boundary, you should speak up for yourself. It's always better to do this calmly. You mustn't let them see your pain. Whatever they say, do not feel blame, shame, or guilt. You know that you can admit when you have made a mistake and apologize. Don't allow people to project their feelings onto you and make you doubt yourself. You are only responsible for your own emotions and your actions.

Lower other expectations.

Even after so much hurt, there's likely a part of you that is still hopeful that they will understand one day. It's time to lower these expectations as a way of self-protection. Stop expecting them to empathize with your situation and stop waiting for that meaningful conversation.

Avoid bringing up the past.

As you have learned about acceptance, this should be easier. What happened in the past should stay there. In the past, you weren't educated on how to deal with a narcissist, so there is little point in bringing up what happened months or years ago. Now that you are more informed, it's best to focus your efforts on the present.

Get the help you need.

If you feel you are going through things you can't cope with, reach out. Your support network is crucial for moving forward in a healthy and positive way. You may have friends or a close family member you can talk with, or you may prefer a therapist. Don't feel you have to suffer alone. As we have seen, personality disorders are far more common than we think, and there is now help available.

What Happens When You Have Tried Everything?

Regardless of gender, ending any relationship is going to be hard. Even though their love for you wasn't real, your love for them certainly was. Even when at rock bottom, there is a small part of your mind and your heart that believes things could be different. The other fear that we may have is not wanting to risk throwing away what we know, just to have the same thing happen again.

It may seem like we are only talking about romantic partnerships, but this applies to all relationships. You can't replace your parents, but you can find fulfilling relationships that will fill you with love and allow you to love.

The first step to breaking free from narcissists is to be absolutely sure you're ready to make the step. One common mistake is the "break up-make up" pattern, which is also seen in non-romantic relationships. You think you have made a decision, then you go back and break away again. Normally, this only prolongs the suffering, and with a narcissist, it definitely will because they won't change. Being absolutely sure of your decision will prevent you from going back.

Next, you need to think of the logistics. If it's a partner, plan out living arrangements and other practicalities. If it's a friend, figure out if you'll be seeing them around mutual friends or if you can avoid them entirely.

What family events will you have to attend together, if any? Is there a way that you can completely distance yourself from your narcissistic coworker? Whenever possible, it's best to make a clean break. If this isn't an option, the contact must be limited to only what is necessary.

Create a fresh list of goals and things you want to achieve. Some ideas include:

• Start a new hobby

• Read a particular book

• Declutter your belongings

• Experience new social events

• Learn a new skill

• Study a course online

• Get more exercise

• Travel

• Get a new haircut/wardrobe

• Advance in your career

This list will help you stay focused and act as a reminder of why you broke away from the person in the first place. It should be filled with all the things you have wanted to do but couldn't.

Prepare what you want to say. Being prepared will help you to feel confident. You don't need a long speech. Let them know that you feel the relationship is no longer healthy and you are going to move on. You do not have to explain your decision. Remember, the more you talk, the more ammunition you give them.

Allow yourself some time to grieve the end of your relationship. It's a process that needs to be worked through in the right way. Don't expect yourself to wake up the next day and feel that life is all better. At the same time, it's important not to get stuck in this period, which is why you should keep your list handy and start ticking off some of your new goals.

Now that you are free from the narcissist, you can start reconnecting with those people with whom you haven't been able to spend time. Ironically, if the narcissist is a parent, this newfound freedom might even allow you to rekindle an old romance. Think about friends from school or college you haven't seen and reach out to them. These people, as well as your current relationships, will act as your support network, particularly while you're building up your strength and getting back on your feet.

An exercise that really helped me was to write a list of all the negative things about my narcissistic people. It was quite extensive, but I made sure I got it all out of my mind and onto paper. I then made every effort to remove reminders of them: photos, gifts, etc. I took a bag, put everything into it, and finally added the list and threw it all away. This provided a great sense of closure.

Focus on the positive things in your life. It will take a while to retrain your brain as you have lived in a swamp of negativity for so long. If you take the time to really look, you'll discover that there are many good things in life. If you're having trouble seeing the good, you might need some therapy—just to give you a little boost in the right direction.

How to Avoid Narcissists in the Future

Through no fault of our own, it's easy to fall for the same behavior that we have been used to. For this reason, you need to give yourself time before jumping into new relationships, regardless of the type. Make sure you give yourself enough time to discover who you really are and what you want from life and your relationships. Dr. Ramani, a licensed clinical psychologist, calls this a deep dive. Look back at what has happened, take what you can from the relationships, and use them to learn more about yourself so you know not to let the same thing happen again.

Dr. Ramani also explains how we store trauma in our bodies. The mind will slowly let go, but there is a very good reason why we should have faith in our gut reactions and the hairs that stand up when we sense something is wrong. There will come a time when you meet new friends, colleagues, and partners. It's wrong to put up your defenses and assume they will treat you in the same way. You aren't being fair or giving them a proper chance. Start each new relationship as a blank slate, but if you feel like you've been down this road before, get out. You want to nip it in the bud early on to protect yourself from the same painful experiences that you've worked so hard to break away from.

So far, we have looked at two of the most toxic types of people. That is not to say that there aren't many other personality types and behaviors we shouldn't have to put up with in our lives. In the next chapter, we'll discuss other types of toxic people who manage to turn our lives upside down.

Putting Chapter 7 into Practice

This is an easy one! Without overthinking, what is the one realistic thing you have always wanted to achieve in your life or the one thing you gave up and wish you hadn't given up because of a toxic relationship? Create a plan to make it happen.

Exercise: The "Empathy Budget"

Think of your empathy like a budget. Each day, decide how much empathy you're willing to spend on the narcissist, and be conscious of when you've hit your limit.

Example:

• "Today, I'm giving them exactly 10% of my energy. No more."

By setting an empathy limit, you'll start noticing how much energy you save for yourself—and you may just realize that the narcissist has been over-budget for years.

Exercise: "Self-Check Phrase"

Pick a go-to phrase you can silently repeat whenever they try to get under your skin. Something like, "This is about them, not me," or "Not my circus, not my monkey." Think of it as your mental shield, a reminder that their behavior isn't your responsibility.

CHAPTER 8: AT TIMES, IT'S NEITHER

 Stop telling the people who do so little for you control so much of your mind, feelings, and emotions.

— *WILL SMITH*

Fortunately, not everyone has a narcissist or sociopath starring in their life story. But that doesn't mean they're off the hook for dealing with toxic behavior.

So far, we have examined extremely toxic people. Unfortunately, there are so many other ways a person can be toxic, so much so that we may fall into the trap of trying to mold our lives around them. Just because someone isn't physically abusing you doesn't mean their behavior gets a free pass!

What exactly does it mean to be toxic? Here's the uncomfortable truth: we all have our moments—you, me, your overly critical neighbor.

But there's a difference between having a toxic moment and being a fully certified toxic person. Knowing where to draw the line is important, so let's get into it.

What Constitutes Toxic Behavior

First things first: the person in your life may not actually be toxic—it could just be their behavior. On the flip side, some people have such a consistently negative impact on your well-being that they might as well come with a "toxic" warning label.

Toxic behavior isn't just anything that rubs you the wrong way or leaves you feeling upset. It's the repeated words, actions, or patterns that chip away at your well-being, stir up unnecessary conflict, and somehow leave you questioning your own sanity. With that definition, it's easy to see how anyone can display toxic behavior from time to time.

Take me, for example. Just last week, I caused a friend a ridiculous amount of stress. I hurt their feelings, totally unintentionally, and yes —I apologized, we moved on, and all was forgiven. But in that moment? I was the problem. I was the one causing the pain. That's toxic behavior, plain and simple. Intentional or not, it happens.

The major difference is that I was able to recognize my actions and make amends, which is what most adults are able to do. Those who display more severe toxic behavior will rarely apologize. Going forward, we'll refer to them as toxic people rather than people with toxic behavior. I don't want you to start feeling guilty and worried because you've upset people—you're not a toxic person!

Toxic people can be manipulators, and their behavior will often confuse you because of a lack of consistency. One minute they'll be happy, the next they may be crying out for attention because their life is so terrible. Not only do you feel uncomfortable around these people, but you also don't feel good about yourself when you are around them.

Toxic people live for drama, and if no drama can be found, they will create it. Overstepping boundaries is just one of the ways they create drama.

Substance abuse can be a problem for toxic people. It doesn't mean that every person who takes drugs or drinks is toxic. But when their behavior starts to negatively impact your life, it also becomes your problem.

Unlike narcissists and sociopaths, toxicity isn't classed as a mental disorder or a personality disorder. That isn't to say that the toxic person doesn't have underlying mental health problems that cause their behavior.

What Is the Difference Between a Bad Day and Toxic Behavior?

To understand the fine line between a bad day and toxic behavior, let's explore some real-life examples and break down when ordinary ups and downs cross into toxicity.

Jane, like many of us, had her share of ups and downs. Health problems, unfortunately, brought her relationship to an end. But she was a fighter, managing to secure both a pay raise and a promotion at work. Whenever she felt low, her friend was there—accompanying her to doctor's appointments, even helping to box up her ex-boyfriend's things and clear him out of her life, literally and figuratively.

But when Jane got that promotion and invited her friend out to celebrate, the calls and messages went unanswered. When she finally did get hold of her, the response was a flat, "Isn't that just great," in a tone that was anything but. Two seconds later, her friend had already moved on, gossiping about someone else.

The next time Jane invited her friend to dinner, eager to talk about a new guy she'd met, the response was a sarcastic, "So soon?" followed by a quick decline. Jane didn't feel like she could say anything—after all, this was the same friend who'd been there when she needed her most.

When we share good news with a friend and they aren't quick to share our joy, it's possible they're dealing with their own problems and are genuinely distracted. Jane's friend, however, crossed the line by downplaying every happy moment Jane had. While she didn't completely ignore Jane's reasons to celebrate, her responses were consistently toxic. Sarcasm is like salt; the right amount makes a dish, but too much and it's ruined. This behavior became toxic as soon as Jane's friend only seemed to benefit from the relationship during times of crisis. A healthy friendship is one where you're there for each other—through the good and the bad.

Let's consider the relationship between Carmen and Mike, who both have full-time jobs. Carmen's job involves a lot of emotional labor, while Mike's is more hands-on and physical. They also juggle responsibilities at home, including caring for their toddler.

After a long day, Carmen often finds herself exhausted, managing her job and household duties. When Mike comes home, he tends to unwind by playing video games or watching TV instead of helping out. One evening, after a particularly challenging day with a sick child, Carmen reached her breaking point. She raised her voice, expressing frustration that Mike wasn't contributing more to their shared responsibilities.

Once things calmed down, Carmen apologized and explained that she needed him to be more engaged. Instead of accepting her apology, Mike dismissed her feelings, saying things like, "You always blow things out of proportion," or "If you managed your time better, you wouldn't be so stressed." He made it seem like Carmen was the problem rather than acknowledging that their workload and responsibilities were unbalanced.

From the outside, it's clear that this dynamic is toxic. However, it can be harder to see when you're in such a relationship like that. Carmen had a tough day and expressed her anger—something we all do from time to time.

In contrast, Mike consistently prioritized his needs over those of their family. He avoided taking responsibility for household duties and judged Carmen's feelings instead of supporting her. This created an imbalance in their relationship.

Both partners should feel valued and supported. Carmen doesn't owe Mike the burden of his hobbies on top of her existing responsibilities. Healthy relationships require both partners to share the load and acknowledge each other's feelings. When one partner repeatedly dismisses the other's needs, it leads to toxicity.

James' sister is a complete control freak. Everything in her life is structured and ordered the way she likes it. There are lists for lists, routines can't be broken, and rules must be obeyed. When she comes to James' apartment, she will move a chair to a slight angle because it looks better. She will bring an air freshener because it smells nicer and rearranges the books by height order. And she is right about everything.

If you try to disagree or show her a different point of view, she will treat you as if you were a child with no experience in the matter. She makes plans for family events, and no one can say no or even make a suggestion. James often finds himself in a position where he has to choose the lesser of two evils just to make sure his sister remains calm, and his parents aren't dragged into discussions.

What James' sister does in her own home is up to her. In all fairness, we all have our little quirks that we either can't change or don't want to. I confess, I also like my books in order of height! Her behavior becomes toxic when she tries to control James' life.

He might be happy to accept that she comes to his place and treats it the same way as her own home, which could be the limit of his boundary. But she crosses the line when James is not allowed to have thoughts, feelings, and opinions of his own. This is a human right that we all should have.

Hannah has a colleague who is generally easy to work with. They collaborate well together, and while they are friendly, there's still a degree of professionalism. Hannah's colleague, Jake, likes to be the center of attention and often has a story to entertain the office.

One day, Hannah noticed that Jake had previously claimed to have lived in Melbourne, but now he was saying he had lived in Sydney for a year. When Hannah questioned him, he said, "Yes, that was before," and she thought nothing more of it. Over time, she noticed a pattern developing, and more and more lies were being told. At first, they were harmless white lies, and the only real damage caused was the inability to trust him.

But then, the lies started creeping into work-related things. He would lie about a report being finished or tell the boss that he had asked Hannah to do something when he hadn't. When he lied to a client, and subsequently, the company lost the client, the whole team suffered.

Trust is a crucial part of any relationship. Without it, we have no foundation to build on. If a colleague is telling lies about their personal life, the professional relationship may not suffer. As soon as Jake started telling lies to and about colleagues, his behavior went from supportable to toxic. This is because his actions created negativity not only for Hannah but also for the others who have to work with him. As well as Hannah not being able to trust him, his lies planted seeds of doubt about who can be trusted in the office.

The main point here is that when you look at these situations and nod your head in agreement, it's rather obvious that the behavior is toxic, possibly even the people. So why is it so hard to spot toxic behavior in our own lives? Simply put, it's because love is blind—even to toxic behavior.

Dealing with Other Elements of Toxicity

Though the prevalence of personality disorders isn't common, 6% globally (Cleveland Clinic, n.d.), there are other sources of toxicity. Psychopaths lack empathy and remorse and are also experts at manipulation. Borderline personality disorder (BPD) is a condition that causes extreme mood swings, impulsive behavior, and low self-esteem. If a person with BPD feels love from a partner, the partner is the hero. If the person doesn't feel love, they are the villain. The ups and downs can be highly toxic for a person living with someone who has BPD.

These emotional extremes are similar to the highs and lows experienced by someone with bipolar disorder, a mental health condition, not a personality disorder. These people can go through everything from emotional highs (known as hypomania) and depression. Toxic behaviors can include impulsivity, lack of empathy, and infidelity.

It might sound extreme, but sarcasm can also be toxic. While the occasional witty, smart comment can add humor to a conversation, there are limits. Sarcasm needs to be used in the right way for it to be funny, and for someone on the receiving end, it can be hurtful. While on the subject of humor, if you notice someone has the habit of turning everything into a joke, this too can be toxic. It's great to be able to find the funny in things, but there are certain situations where this is inappropriate, especially if the use of humor opens old emotional wounds.

Another trait that can be good in moderation is competitiveness. It has the potential to motivate and drive people to push themselves, but not everything should be approached as a competition. Competitiveness can be incredibly subtle, but when someone isn't happy with your achievements, it's often a sign that their competitiveness is unhealthy.

Here is one final incredibly subtle toxic behavior you might be guilty of— the need to fix everyone and everything. The desire to help others leads to a strong determination to rescue or fix people. There is no doubt that wanting to help people is an admirable trait, but when taken too far, it's easy to feel that other people's lives have become our responsibility. Subtle toxic behaviors aren't just about what others do to us but also what we do to ourselves.

Over the years, I have noticed that some people will use the words "toxic" and "abusive" interchangeably, and while there are overlaps, there are also a couple of differences, and most of them come down to control. An abuser will always need to be in control in all areas of their relationship, from sex to finances. They will also want to manage aspects of the other person's life, like who they see and what they can do. Abusers use bullying tactics, and each move or decision is well-calculated. Abusive behavior doesn't change, whereas, with the right tools and knowledge, toxic behavior can.

What Can You Do When Love Is Causing Blindness to Toxicity?

For those closest to us—our long-term partners, best friends, parents, and siblings—it isn't always so easy. In many cases, we have had these people in our lives for so long that we accept that this is who they are. In other cases, our love is so blind that we don't even see it.

One of the biggest problems with toxic behavior in those closest to us is that it can appear gradually and subtly. Take your family, for example. While growing up, you may not recognize how much your parents' toxic behavior impacted you until you reach adulthood. Your sibling probably used to be your best friend, but as you both start to mold your own lives, they may have been caught up in a circle of toxic people, and it does rub off. Bit by bit, you begin to notice changes in them, and it has a greater impact on your relationship.

When you're with friends, you might start noticing little things that bug you, things you wish could change. It's not until you are in a seriously bad situation together that you realize just how toxic they can be. For example, when your car breaks down in the middle of nowhere, instead of helping, they make things worse by complaining or bailing.

Let's take a look at three specific relationships and how you can spot the most subtle signs of toxic behavior. Remember that some points may apply to all of your closest relationships.

How to spot subtle toxic behavior from your family:

• You are constantly walking on eggshells around them

• There are many arguments, and they make these arguments personal

• They don't accept your sexual preferences

• They don't accept your choice of partner

• They don't respect your opinions or beliefs

- They tell you how to raise your children

- You feel you do things only for their approval

- Your family frequently disappoints you

- They are violent toward you

- They are controlling, expecting you to do what the rest of the family is doing

Ways to know if your friends are toxic:

- They constantly cancel plans or don't show up

- You start to dread social occasions with them

- They bring up your biggest insecurity right after they compliment you

- You are sad, upset, and stressed after social occasions with them

- They drink too much and become aggressive or insult you

- They make you feel guilty for doing what you want to do

- They gossip about you

- You feel like you need a nap after every conversation with them, even though you just had three cups of coffee

- They post negative things about you on social media

- You are never thanked for the things you do for them

- You feel like you are being bullied

- They don't respect your personal space

When love stops you from seeing your partner's toxic behavior:

- You can't communicate without arguing, being bitter, or sarcastic

- There is a lack of support

- You start to feel jealousy and resentment

• Your partner makes important financial decisions without talking to you first

• You have lost other important relationships for fear of upsetting your partner

• You have stopped taking care of yourself, both your mental and physical health

• You don't have time for your hobbies

• In your mind, you keep telling yourself it's a phase and things will change

• You find yourself telling lies so that you don't have to spend more time with them

• They ridicule you in front of friends and family

• There is no balance or equality, a shared understanding of who does what

What is highly dangerous about subtle toxic behavior is that it is contagious. Toxic people often lie, but then you find yourself telling lies to avoid confrontation. How many times have you seen online bullying be retaliated with more bullying?

Even with subtle toxic behavior, you can only take responsibility for your own actions and emotions. And as harsh as it sounds, you have to learn how to stop putting yourself in situations where those closest to you can keep causing pain.

Change Is Possible

After taking off the blinkers and seeing things for how they really are, you are now ready to start taking some small steps to see the necessary changes.

We like to start with the smaller steps because this way, you gain confidence and knowing you can do it makes it easier to tackle harder situations.

1. Don't bring up the past

It's not as simple as "forgive and forget" because the pain people cause stays with us. If your partner is unfaithful, you can't just put it in the past and trust again. When we talk about putting things in the past, it's about not bringing past actions into present conversations. It won't be productive and is more likely to cause tension in the conversation. It's important to focus on the present and the changes you want to see.

2. Get to the bottom of their issues

They might not even be aware of their toxic behavior or the extent to which it is damaging the relationship. Their behavior will stem from some root cause. Make it clear that you do not excuse the way they treat you, but being understanding and helping them work through their issues can reduce the toxicity and strengthen the relationship.

Of course, if they are unwilling to accept the problems, you will struggle to see the changes you need.

3. Focus on accountability rather than blaming

People find it hard to admit they made a mistake or have done something wrong. We sometimes mistake being accountable for admitting to our failings and weaknesses. It's easier to highlight the faults of others and blame them. Even though you're working to prevent the other person's toxic behavior, taking your fair share of the blame for those bad days that turn into toxic acts is good practice. It's a little bit like you're showing them that it's okay to be accountable and how to say sorry when necessary.

Nevertheless, never apologize for things that aren't your fault, and don't allow yourself to be manipulated into saying sorry.

4. Say no to toxic behavior

I know you might feel hesitant to confront the situation, but now is the best time to put a stop to being treated like a doormat. You don't deserve to be treated with anything less than love and respect. When people treat you in a way that causes you to suffer, call them out on this behavior and tell them that it isn't right. Choose the best time to do this. You should make sure you are emotionally calm, and if you're worried about the other person's reaction, do it in a public place or with people around you that you can trust.

5. Set boundaries

Boundaries are essential when dealing with all toxic people. It's another way of letting people know that there are certain things that you will not tolerate—no matter what.

When you have decided on your boundaries, you need to make sure that they are clearly communicated. Because toxic people often try to cross boundaries, you'll have to keep repeating yourself and showing that you are serious by following through with the consequences when your boundaries are crossed. As soon as you don't reinforce a boundary, the toxic person will find a way to revert to old habits.

6. Take care of yourself

If you feel like you have been putting yourself in second place, now is also the time to change this. Others will continue to disregard your needs and place their own ahead of yours until you remind them that your well-being is equally important. Look after yourself by taking time to do the things you want to do, whether that's exercise, a trip to the movies, or going to a particular restaurant. Don't wait for your loved one to agree to come with you. There's something incredibly empowering about doing these things alone—it's not the same as being lonely!

7. Allow some time to see the changes

As long as both of you are actively working to improve, the right changes will come about, but it won't be overnight. You are working to change behavior that is well-established, possibly over the years. It's like learning to drive on the right-hand side of the road, and then all of a sudden, you have to drive on the left. Each day gets easier, but there might be some minor setbacks along the way.

Remember that you have to see the changes and not just hear that they will happen.

8. Decide on the level of contact you are happy with

Generally speaking, you can decide on one of three levels of contact. First, you can remove yourself from situations when the person shows toxic behavior. For example, if your best friend becomes toxic after drinking too much, you can refuse to go out with them. Second, you can decide that minimal contact is best. This means you would only see family members at group occasions, weddings, funerals, etc. Third, you can go with no contact at all. This is obviously going to be the most difficult due to how close the relationship is. If minimal contact is still upsetting you too much, you might want to set a period of time with no contact. This could be a month, a few months, or even a year. During this time, you can analyze if your life is better or worse without them in it. It's then up to you to decide if you want to reconnect and whether the person has made any significant changes during the no-contact period.

Real-World Examples of How These Strategies Can Be Successful

To put these strategies into practice, let's take the same examples we saw with Jane, Carmen, James, and Hannah and see how things could have turned out if they had known how to handle toxic behavior.

Jane and the drama-seeking friend

People looking for drama often do so because they are seeking a distraction from their own reality. Our own problems are usually so difficult to resolve that we may feel helpless. But when we see other people in turmoil, it's easier to see the solution. Drama seekers often do so because they can't find solutions to their own problems. Being there during other people's drama keeps them busy, and they feel like they are involved in a solution.

Here, the loved one is only there when you're going through problems. You need to take time to put your problems to one side (temporarily) so that you can try to help this person resolve what is upsetting them. Considering the prevalence of toxicity, they may be trying to deal with their own toxic people.

Jane's best option would have been to shift the focus onto her friend and allow the friend to open up about what is bothering them. Even the toxic words that came out as sarcasm could have been because of her friend's personal problems.

This is what is known as extending an olive branch. You are providing an opportunity for the loved one to explain their behavior, which might be the chance for them to realize that they are in the wrong.

If they don't open up about what is bothering them or they tell you that there is nothing wrong, you need to let them know that their actions and words have hurt you and that in the future, you expect to enjoy both the highs and the lows with your friend.

Carmen and the needy partner

Although getting angry wasn't the best solution, it is not the root of the problem. Carmen and Mike have communication issues, and it's become so bad that Mike has become toxic and Carmen is slowly picking up more toxic behavior.

To break the cycle, Mike and Carmen need to have an open conversation. It's best to do this when neither is tired, and there is someone to take care of their toddler so that they aren't distracted.

The conversation should focus on "I" sentences instead of "You." Sentences that start with "I" focus the attention on your feelings. Sentences that start with "You" can sound like blame. Look at the difference between "I feel hurt when you don't do your share" compared with "You hurt me when you don't do your share."

The conversation should also include a plan for running the home on a more equal basis. Carmen also needs to dedicate some time to herself so that Mike can't accuse her of being jealous. Finally, Carmen will have to be patient, and they should celebrate their wins together.

James and the controlling sister

One of the most common causes of controlling behavior is anxiety disorder. We know the feeling of a crazy world where nothing seems to be in our control—it's stressful, but for some, it becomes too much, and they find peace in controlling everything they can. James can try to be more understanding of her feelings and perhaps encourage her to get professional help for her problems.

If his sister refuses, he will have to set firm boundaries and let his sister know what will happen if she crosses the line. James will also need to decide on an appropriate level of contact so that he protects himself if his sister can't change.

Hannah and the lying colleague

There are many reasons why people lie. It might be to avoid embarrassment, to protect someone else from getting hurt, or to feel better about themselves. As we mentioned before, there is a fine line between the odd white lie about your experiences and a full-blown lie. The minute that Hannah's colleague crossed that line, Hannah should have called him out on it so that he was aware that the workspace does not tolerate lies.

Another very important thing, particularly in a workplace, is to document everything. Every message, email, and lie should be kept in a file. It might sound dramatic, but HR should have a copy of the file if there is any risk to your position or career. Encouraging other colleagues to do the same is a good idea so that one bad apple doesn't spoil the whole basket.

They Don't Deserve Endless Chances Though

Relationships and our experiences are subjective. What one person might see as toxic could be very different from the next person, and only two people ever really know what goes on in a relationship. Other people's advice can be welcoming, but only you can make the final decision as to whether or not there is a future.

I will, however, urge you to strongly consider ending any relationship where you feel your life is in danger (and this applies to your children too) or, at the very least, to get some professional help, whether that's from law enforcement or other support networks.

Here are a few signs that might indicate that you have tried and given them enough chances.

• They continue to put you down

• They pressure you to do things you don't want to

• They are still attempting to manipulate you

• You don't feel supported

• They don't celebrate your successes

• Their negativity drains you

• They don't respect your feelings

• There is no give-and-take

• They continue to lie

• They still always have to be right

Bear in mind that all of your logical side will be telling you that you should leave, and your emotional side is starting to get on board, yet there is still something holding you back. It's perfectly normal to fear ending a toxic relationship, but know that you are, even if you can't see it right now, much stronger than you imagine.

The range of toxicity levels is huge. Toxic behavior can be minor little things that really get to you, or they can be major ones that are now starting to take over your life. Nobody's situation will be exactly the same, and each of us has our own personality. For this reason, there isn't a one-fix solution for toxic behavior.

This chapter has provided some of the most effective solutions to help overcome such issues with those closest to you. Once again, I have purposely not discussed manipulation. All toxic behavior comes from manipulation. We will dedicate the next chapter to the prevalence of manipulation in today's world and take a deep dive into the dark psychology behind it.

Putting Chapter 8 into Practice

Again, this is a moment for observation before taking steps. Just because you don't have a sociopath or a narcissist in your life doesn't mean you aren't suffering. Step outside the home and consider all of your relationships. Look for subtle things that may have dragged you down in the past but blamed yourself for and take a moment for self-reflection in case of subtle toxic behaviors of your own. When you know what you are dealing with, you will be prepared to take action.

CHAPTER 9: THE REAL PROBLEM: MANIPULATION

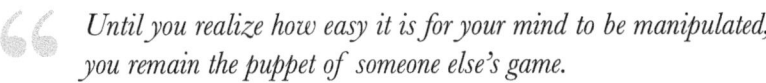 *Until you realize how easy it is for your mind to be manipulated, you remain the puppet of someone else's game.*

— *EVITA OCHEL*

Years ago, I felt like such an idiot, and time and time again, I thought, "Man, I have been played again." I was completely unable to see when I was being manipulated, and I definitely couldn't see it coming.

Toxic behavior and manipulation are best friends walking down the street together. They bounce off each other, fuel each other, and creep up on you without you being aware. It's perfectly normal for us not to notice when we are being manipulated, mainly because nobody wants to think that our friends and family are capable of such techniques.

What Is Manipulation?

"Manipulation is the act of controlling someone or something to your own advantage, often unfairly or dishonestly" (Cambridge

Dictionary, 2021). When we talk about controlling people, it could be their emotions, perceptions, behavior, and/or relationships.

Remember how we mentioned our habit of saying we're fine or okay when people ask how we are? This is also a form of manipulation because we are controlling how people perceive us. Instead of seeing us as sad, angry, or depressed, they see us as okay. Most of us do this, so there is no need to start worrying that you are a chronic manipulator. This is a common reaction that is not designed to try and gain personally but to prevent others from becoming concerned.

Some examples of manipulation include:

• Lying or withholding information

• Threatening or implying threats

• Isolating people from their loved ones

• Passive aggression

• Verbal abuse

• Intellectual bullying

• Gaslighting

• Using sex to get what they want

• Creating an imbalance of power

• Negative surprises to catch you off guard

• The silent treatment

• Playing the victim

The reasons behind people's manipulative behavior can be unconscious, but it can also reach the other extreme and be completely malicious and intentional.

Victims can be left exhausted both physically and mentally as they try to please these people. They might begin to suffer from anxiety or depression. Not only may they start lying about their emotions, but they might also start to find it incredibly hard to develop trusting relationships.

The manipulator may also have their own mental health issues that are causing this toxic behavior. Narcissists and sociopaths frequently use manipulation and are fully aware of their behavior.

People who have been diagnosed with borderline personality may manipulate others in order to have their needs met. But there doesn't have to be a mental health diagnosis to engage in manipulative tactics. It can also be because a person is scared or anxious and needs to control all of their surroundings.

Why Is Manipulation So Toxic?

There are plenty of examples in the world where manipulation is considered perfectly normal, so much so that we don't even consider being manipulated.

Marketing and advertising use manipulative techniques to convince us to choose particular products or services. This might sound like a trivial example but imagine the cleaning product or toothpaste that you always use—and for good reason. But an ad catches your attention and you decide to try the new product. The cleaning product could be useless or the toothpaste disgusting. But the company managed to change your purchasing behavior for its own gain.

If you look at this example in a non-marketing context, the theory is the same. You make a decision based on your knowledge and your gut.

Despite knowing it's the right choice, somebody can use psychology to change your mind. As what they want goes against your original instincts, it's often not in your best interest and, therefore, harms you. Manipulation in relationships can become so toxic that the result is a breakdown in that relationship. Let's take a look at an example.

Meet Emily and Tom. They've been dating for about nine months. The honeymoon phase? Still going strong. He's charming, attentive, and always knows how to make her laugh. They've even got that cute couple banter that makes their friends roll their eyes. Everything's going great—or so Emily thinks.

One evening, Emily mentioned that she had been invited to a big networking event for work. She's excited, maybe even a little nervous, and shares the news with Tom. His reaction? *"Oh, so you're really going to leave me alone all night?"*

Although he says it with a smile, there's something about his tone that feels a little off. She brushes it aside, convinced he's just being playful. After all, he's been nothing but supportive, right?

Fast-forward a few weeks, and the same pattern emerges. Emily makes plans for happy hour with her coworkers—*"Wow, you must really need a break from me,"* Tom jokes, a half-smile on his face. Emily laughs it off again.

But soon, it's happening with every plan she makes. Dinner with friends becomes a guilt trip. A family weekend turns into a passive-aggressive sigh-fest. Tom's not *forbidding* her from going out—he's just *gently* making her feel like a bad girlfriend for wanting any life outside of their relationship.

There was no particular red flag for Emily because it crept up on her slowly. Tom used the pretense of love and affection to subtly control her life, and before she knew it, Emily mistook his need for control as genuine care. This kind of manipulation isn't gender-specific—both men and women are capable of manipulating their friends, partners, and even colleagues in ways that are hard to spot until it's too late.

What Do Manipulators Have in Common?

Although people manipulate in various ways, manipulators have a certain number of techniques and traits in common. Understanding these will help you to recognize the signs earlier and be better prepared.

1. They can't just ask for what they need

I prefer to be straightforward when I need help from a friend, and I've been working on being more emotionally aware so that I can respect their response. People who manipulate will never ask for help directly because it means giving up their control. Instead, they use psychological tactics to control others and say things like, "I've just been so overwhelmed lately, and no one seems to care how hard things are for me." They play the victim to get you to offer help without having to ask for it.

2. They are expert gaslighters

Gaslighting is one of the most painful forms of manipulation because you start to question your own reality and sanity. If you ask your partner to do the shopping and they don't, they might turn around and say that you never asked them. Manipulators will use subtle phrases like, "Are you sure you're feeling alright?" to "You're just being crazy," both of which will make you question what has really happened.

3. They project their emotions

Projection is when you displace your own feelings onto another person. In most cases, it's a defense mechanism, but manipulators use it to shift the blame for their own negative emotions. Examples could be an angry manipulator accusing their victim of always being angry or a cheating partner who starts to suspect their partner is also cheating.

4. They make generalizations

Generalizations can hurt because the manipulator doesn't take the time or effort to understand what you are truly saying. Imagine if Dad had a problematic day at work and explains the details to Mom. When the kids ask what's wrong with Dad, Mom says, "He's in a mood again." This is a general statement that makes Dad look bad in front of the kids when, in reality, he has a lot on his plate.

5. They have an inappropriate, nasty sense of humor

Really, it's a little bit like bullying, but if you feel like you're always at the end of a joke and these jokes hurt your feelings, you're dealing with a manipulator. In front of the others, they are just being funny, engaging in a bit of innocent humor. However, they are fully aware that their joke causes you pain, and they might even rub salt in the wound by telling you that you are too sensitive.

6. They divide and conquer

Manipulators have no problems being extra friendly to a person and then talking down about them to others. This technique is used to control how others see you. It's particularly dangerous in groups of friends or with colleagues. Manipulators will also tell you what others are saying about you, often lying or exaggerating.

7. They don't stay on topic

As soon as it looks like a manipulator will have to own their emotions or actions, they'll change the subject. This is sometimes harder to spot because it seems so innocent but they are doing it to avoid accountability.

8. They will always be dissatisfied with you

No matter if you do everything they require or reach the necessary goals, they will move the goalposts and expect more. You will find that you are constantly trying to prove yourself to them and never meeting expectations.

After reading these descriptions, you might suddenly become aware that you are being manipulated and, from personal experience, feel angry at yourself. Don't be. These people have been practicing these techniques for years—it's second nature to them. What matters now is that you're wise to their behavior.

Spotting Manipulative Phrases

If you find it challenging to identify manipulative behavior, which is perfectly natural at first, there are some phrases that are commonly used.

• "I never said that."

• "You shouldn't feel like that."

• "You shouldn't think like that."

• "You're being dramatic."

• "You're overreacting."

• "You made me do it."

• "I said sorry. What else do you want from me?"

• "You're being sensitive."

• "You're being paranoid."

• "I was only joking."

• "You're imagining things."

• "Everyone thinks I'm right."

Let's put a few of these phrases into context. When someone denies saying something, it's possible that they never said what you think they said.Before accusing someone of manipulating you, make sure you are 100% sure they didn't say or do what you think they did. If there's any doubt that you may have misunderstood or if the message wasn't clear, ask for clarification.If you know that they are manipulating you, you'll be able to find strategies to handle this in the next chapter.

The Dark Psychology of Manipulation

Dark psychology focuses on the science of manipulation and control, a subject that psychologists and even criminologists use to understand problems arising from manipulation. The Dark Triad is a set of three harmful and toxic personality profiles: narcissism, psychopathy, and Machiavellianism (Paulhus & Williams, 2002). Although we've touched on The Dark Triad previously, it needs more attention in terms of manipulation. To elaborate, the Dark Triad is:

Narcissism: the inflated ego, a lack of empathy, a superior sense of self

Psychopathy: charming and kind, but selfish and devoid of remorse

Machiavellianism: using manipulation to exploit others with no sense of morals

The Dark Triad sounds so severe that you would assume it's a type of manipulation that is less common, but it is quite the contrary. Here are some ways people use Dark Triad traits in everyday situations:

• **Love flooding or sucking up:** giving gifts, compliments, and affection before asking someone for something.

• **Telling lies:** telling partial truths, exaggerations, or just flat-out lies.

• **Withholding love and affection:** a lack of interest in the person to withholding physical contact, hugs, kisses, and sex.

• **Restricting choices:** offering two or more choices but none of them is the choice the person actually wants to make.

• **Reverse psychology:** Telling someone not to do something to encourage them to want to do it, or vice versa.

• **Using semantics:** Many words have more than one meaning depending on the context; a person can use one definition, and while the understanding is clear, the manipulator will purposely use the other meaning.

Dark psychology and the Dark Triad are quite common. Some

people do not make any effort to avoid such behavior but actually teach it, for example, in some sales and marketing companies. This is the extent to which some will go to ensure their goals and needs are met above all else.

Am I Being Manipulated? Can I Avoid It?

Perhaps you have your suspicions, but you can't definitely say yes or no just yet. Being sure of yourself is the first step in understanding the principles of manipulation so that you can identify it when it occurs before it's too late.

Ask yourself the questions below. Try to be firm with yourself and only answer with yes or no. If we answer on a scale or include "maybes," we open the door to excuses for their behavior.

1. Is the situation your responsibility?

2. Will you feel good about making your decision?

3. Are you doing it to avoid feeling emotionally overwhelmed?

4. Are you scared to say no?

5. Are there any strings attached?

6. Would the other person do the same for you if the situation were reversed?

7. Is your gut telling you this is right?

You shouldn't feel obliged to do anything you don't want to do, and we all have the right to say no. If you feel something isn't in your best interest, you have to put the brakes on straight away. Boundaries and saying no are the best ways to avoid manipulation, but these aren't skills that come naturally to everyone. For this reason, we'll take a deeper look at enhancing these essential skills a little later on.

One very simple way to avoid being manipulated is to share your intentions. The more people know how you feel, what you're doing, and what your goals are, the harder it is for manipulators to control how others view you. You should also make sure that everything is documented and that you share this with others too. A manipulator in the office can't deny their responsibilities when you have sent an email telling everyone the steps you are about to take toward the office goal.

On a similar note, expand your support group. The more knowledgeable people you have in your support group, the harder it becomes for a manipulator to isolate you. What's more, with an extended group of kind, positive people around you, you can discuss and share ideas and opinions freely. This is a great strategy for increasing your perspectives and finding faith in your gut instincts.

Finally, be strong, confident, and firm. Tell the manipulator that you're aware of what they're trying to achieve and you won't tolerate it. Keep it factual rather than emotional because it's harder to deny things when there is evidence to support it. Manipulators aren't used to being called out on their behavior, so confrontation is likely, but their reaction is not your responsibility. Remember to keep your goals in mind and be proud of yourself for doing something many would just ignore.

How to Avoid Manipulating Others

In the effort to be completely accountable, it's only fair to reflect on our own behaviors and ensure that we are also not unintentionally manipulating others. Again, this isn't a sign that you are a toxic person. Manipulation can be a learned behavior, so if you grew up in a home where manipulation was common, you may not even realize you're doing it. For example, deflecting blame in an argument, needing to know where people are all the time, and expecting others to know how you feel without communicating are all forms of manipulation, albeit more subtle.

In some cases, manipulative behaviors stem from a need to be in control, and when you aren't in control, you start to feel anxious. A need for control often comes from low self-esteem, which is a great place to start. You deserve to have time to explore your hobbies and passions and discover what you excel at. Once you identify your strengths, you can begin to tame the inner critic and talk to yourself with more kindness and compassion.

For your anxiety, engage in mindfulness and meditation. Find things that bring you peace, whether curling up with a good book or spending time in nature. If you notice that your anxiety stems from perfectionism, it's essential that you let go of the idea that everything has to be perfect. There are just too many things in life beyond your control, and attempting to can only lead to more anxiety. An awesome affirmation for this is, "It's not perfect, but it's better."

Finally, learn how to listen to other people's thoughts and feelings. You may think you're paying attention, but ask yourself if you're formulating a response in your head or if you're genuinely listening to the complete message.

Effective communication is about both parties feeling understood, and this has to go both ways. Just as you wouldn't want people assuming they know how you feel, don't assume you know what they're going through. Conflict is a given, but respecting the other person, their right to finish expressing themselves, and the right to their own beliefs and opinions can help you see things from their perspective rather than relying on learned behaviors.

Avoiding the manipulator and their tactics is one thing. Knowing you are ahead of the game and have protected yourself is empowering. If the manipulator has made their way into your life and you aren't sure how to cope with them, we can still put a stop to it and even come out better on the other side. Our next chapter focuses on what to do when you can't avoid a manipulative person.

Putting Chapter 9 into Practice

It's possible you are still doubting whether someone is manipulating you or not. This is the time to pay attention to how a person's words make you feel. If someone tells you they were just joking, do you feel a sense of relief, or do you feel like you have been made a fool of? Do you feel like the requests you receive are fair, or does a request cause you to feel frustrated? Pay close attention to these feelings because they aren't signs of being overly sensitive; they are your emotions alerting you that something isn't right.

Exercise: The "Flip the Script" Test

Here's a quick gut check for when someone's request or "joke" leaves you squirming: Flip it around. Imagine you said or asked the same thing of them. How would they react? Would they laugh it off or comply easily? Or would they suddenly get defensive?

Example:

• "If I told them, 'I was only joking' after a critical comment, would they laugh or feel hurt?"

• "If I asked them to cancel plans to help me, would they even consider it?"

This little exercise is a quick way to see if they're playing fair or just playing you. Often, manipulators have one set of rules for you and a different set for themselves. If their behavior only goes one way, that's your sign.

CHAPTER 10: BEATING MANIPULATION

Now that we understand just how common manipulation is, it's clear that we can't avoid it entirely.

Preventing yourself from being subjected to these tactics would involve cutting yourself off from many people in your life, never meeting new people, and, of course, turning off all social media, news, ads, etc. Not only is this unhealthy, but you are also missing out on so many potentially wonderful experiences and relationships.

The fact is, it's okay to have manipulative people in your life as long as you know how to handle them and don't end up being controlled and dictated by them.

That doesn't mean carrying on as if nothing happened. Learning the essential skills to spot and stop manipulation is how you will take back the power over your own life and start to enjoy yourself more.

This chapter offers seven powerful tactics to show your manipulator that their behavior will not be tolerated.

But before that, let's just make sure we haven't missed any manipulative signs.

Recognizing Long-Term Manipulation

In the previous chapter, we spent a considerable amount of time reviewing how to spot manipulation before it occurs. You probably also have a good sense of when people you can't avoid are trying to manipulate you. Manipulation can be covert or overt, so either very subtle or completely self-directed. It's the act of using psychology to control others into feeling or acting in ways that go against their true self.

When we have been around a person for a long time, manipulation often blends in with other toxic behaviors, and it's not so easy to detect. Whether intentional or not, manipulators might rely on the most subtle of ways to slowly break you down. These are the most difficult to spot, especially when it involves those closest to you.

Aside from what we discussed in the previous chapter, a red flag should be waved if you notice that a person always encourages you to speak first. Although it may seem like they're just being polite, they might actually be trying to establish a baseline for your thoughts. They may even follow up with some questions, which again, seems considerate, but their intention may be for you to open up so they can find your weaknesses and then cultivate their own plan.

You should also be wary of people who always decide on the meeting place, regardless of the activity. You might want dinner here, they want it there; you want to shop at X, but they want Y; you suggest hanging out at your house, but they insist it has to be theirs. We are tempted to go along with these plans so as not to rock the boat, but they are trying to draw you out of your comfort zone and force you into locations where they have control.

There are also forms of passive-aggressive behavior that shouldn't be tolerated. One of the classics is playing dumb. This can be with any range of activities, from not knowing how to work the washing machine to not understanding your tax returns or being unable to figure out a new piece of technology. By playing dumb, the person manipulates you to do it for them because it's easier and quicker if you do it rather than explain things.

The guilt trip is another form of passive-aggressive behavior. This can appear playful at times—the bottom lip pout, a smile, and saying, "If you loved me, you would do it." A harsher form of guilt trip is to accuse others of being selfish or not caring in order to fulfill their demands.

Finally, we go back to intellectual bullying. Bombardments of facts and statistics create a sense that they know more than you do. They will then give you very little time to make a decision. Both of these tactics are because they want their own agenda to be followed instead of allowing you time to look at things from alternative points of view. This doesn't have to be only in the workplace. Friends or family can throw information at you when planning events—highlighting reasons why their plan is superior and then saying a decision has to be made immediately so that the booking can be made.

If you feel like you're acting or speaking in ways that go against who you really are or if you feel constantly drained or confused by a particular person, you will want to begin working on the following techniques to start seeing impressive changes.

7 Powerful Tactics to Overcome Manipulation

1. Know and stand up for your fundamental human rights

There are 30 basic human rights according to the Universal Declaration of Human Rights (United Nations, 1948). Some that are subject to manipulation are the right to equality in marriage, the right to own things, the freedom of thought and religion, and the freedom of opinion and expression. You also have the right to privacy.

The very first human right is that all human beings are free and equal. Nobody deserves more or less than the next person. Nobody is superior, despite how they feel or how society paints them. That being said, as we are all free to have our own opinions, the manipulator has the right to feel superior, but it's not right for them to make others feel inferior. Article 30 states that human rights can't be taken away, which is the key to our understanding. No matter what others try to do, you have rights.

2. Keep your distance as best you can

Just because you spend eight hours a day with a colleague, live with your significant other, or are close to your family, it doesn't mean you have to feel obligated to constantly be by their side. Put some distance between you and the person and only spend the necessary time with them. Taking this step can help you gain confidence, strength, and control during the time apart, which will help you handle them in those moments you can't avoid.

3. Stop blaming yourself

There are two main categories of things we blame ourselves for: things we shouldn't feel guilty about and things that should be left in the past. You shouldn't blame yourself for your emotions or your needs. They are what they are. If you feel tired, happy, sad, or fed up, just own it and remember that people don't have the right to judge you. They also don't have the right to make you feel bad because you need a night in to recuperate or want a night out to have fun.

It's common for us to blame ourselves when we can't do something right or if we aren't good at something. Humans aren't supposed to be perfect. Instead of blaming yourself for what you can't do, focus on what you do well, and don't feel guilty for being proud of this.

If you have been hurt by someone you trusted, or there has been an end to a relationship, these things aren't going to change. It is crucial that we learn from our past but don't allow ourselves to keep reliving it (huffpost.com).

I know all of this is easier said than done, particularly if someone in your life constantly reminds you of what they consider to be failings.

Following steps 1 and 2 will help you stop manipulators from seeing this self-blame as a weakness they can use.

4. Turn the focus back on the manipulator

Whether the manipulator is aware of their behavior or not, turning the focus back on them will allow them to see their wrongdoings or shock them into realizing you are onto their behavior. To do this, you need to ask them probing questions:

• Does this seem fair to you?

• Is what you're asking of me reasonable?

• Do I have a say in the matter?

• Are you asking me or telling me?

• What am I going to get out of this?

• Are you honestly expecting me to (restate their request)?

• Have you taken my time into consideration?

• Have you taken my opinion into consideration?

The sad fact is that a manipulator won't care about the responses to these questions because their only concern is achieving their goals. Fairness, your opinion and time, or what you will get out of it wouldn't cross their mind. On the other hand, if someone is genuinely interested in your well-being, they will take a moment to answer the questions honestly.

5. Set and establish firm consequences

Most of us have boundaries, even if we aren't fully aware that this is what they are. Our boundaries are our individual set of rules that we live by. This code of conduct comes from our values and beliefs as well as past experiences that we don't want to happen again. People's boundaries are very personal, but most of us would agree that committing a crime is a line we wouldn't cross, along with discrimination, bullying, cheating, and invading personal space. If you aren't 100% clear on what your boundaries are, you must define them now before you try to set them. Take a moment to think about past situations that have hurt you. At what point did it become too much? A peck on the cheek is one thing, but lingering there might have made you feel uncomfortable, so you're clear that this is a boundary for you.

In most personal and professional relationships, people will understand your boundaries and respect them. For a manipulator, there is no such thing as boundaries, and they will happily violate them if their needs are met.

When a person insists on crossing a line and making you feel uncomfortable, their behavior becomes toxic. To show the seriousness of boundary violations, you have to have consequences ready. For example, if a colleague is overstepping the line with physical contact, you need to tell them that if it happens again, you will report them to HR. If a family member or partner gets angry, verbally or physically abusive, let them know that you will walk away from the situation and the relationship if necessary. When friends are constantly late or don't show up, inform them that you won't make plans with them in the future.

Consequences are incredibly valuable, but only if you enforce them. For example, if your partner is yelling at you and you don't walk away, the manipulator will learn that they can continue with their negative behavior and that your boundaries don't mean anything. Only set a consequence if you know you can follow through with it.

To get better at setting boundaries and their consequences, practice what you want to say beforehand to be more confident and articulate.

6. Learn to say NO—and practice it regularly

Saying no is tough for many different reasons. The most common is that we don't want to let people down or are afraid of the other person's reaction. Another less discussed reason is that we don't like the idea that we can't do everything that is required of us. Not being able to juggle work, family life, and a social life can make us feel as if we are failing at something. Despite all of this, saying no is crucial for our mental and physical well-being, putting our needs first and reinforcing those boundaries. It's important to remember that saying no isn't a bad thing at all, but it does take practice and determination. There are a few handy tips to bear in mind when saying no:

• Decide whether you want to say yes or no—if you aren't sure, ask for more time.

• Be kind in your no, not just with the words but also with your tone and body language.

• Thank the person for considering you.

• Offer an alternative that suits you both.

• Be prepared to have to say a firmer no.

Let's expand on this with an example. Samantha's family wants her to bring her children on vacation for two weeks during the summer. Her parents have applied a bit of a guilt trip, saying that they never get to spend time with the grandkids, and who knows how much longer they'll be around! Here are two ways that Samantha could reply:

1. "Thanks for the offer. It would be a lovely trip, but I can't commit as we have plans already. We could do a week, though."

2. "No, I'm sorry. That's not going to work for me."

You can see that the first sentence is the softer way of saying no without actually having to use the word. The second sentence is firmer but still not rude or aggressive. We sometimes need to start with the kinder words and use firmer words if the person pushes back.

These are effective steps for saying no to the average person, but they might not be sufficient for the manipulators in our lives. It's rarely a good idea to explain to a manipulator why you are saying no because they will use your words against you and try to change your schedule so that you have no excuse to say no. Here are some straight-to-the-point phrases you can use to reject a demand from a manipulator.

-Thank you, but no.

-My timetable won't allow for that.

-It's not going to work for me.

-No, I can't.

-I'm too busy today, but I'm free tomorrow.

-I'm not comfortable with that.

-I have a rule not to…

-No!

-I have said no, and I meant it.

There's a chance that the person you are saying no to will get angry or create a scene. This is on them and not you. You have said no in a firm but fair way, and you don't need to justify this answer or feel guilty about it. If the person's reaction is too much for you to handle, let them know you are leaving and will talk about it again once they have calmed down.

7. Confront the bully for what they are—in the right way

Nobody wants to feel like they're being pushed around or walked all over. You can only take so much before a very unexpected and out-of-character outburst occurs. While it might feel good to get it all off your chest, when dealing with a manipulator, it's more likely that it will backfire, suggesting that you are out of control or even crazy. This is why you have to make sure that you are confronting your bully in the right way: safely, calmly, and intelligently. For this to take place, there has to be enough time to have a conversation.

Both parties need to be in the right frame of mind, and most of all, it needs to be calm. It's better to wait if you don't feel like you can control your emotions at the time. If you fear for your safety in any way, make sure that there are people around you in case things turn aggressive or violent. Your safety isn't worth sacrificing just to confront a bully, so choose the time wisely.

Not everyone is out to manipulate you, but life will become more pleasant when you can identify the behavior and master how to handle it. Those who care about you will take on board what you are saying. The changes won't occur overnight as you are changing habits that have been in place for a long time, but you will start to see the efforts bear fruit. Don't forget that a little bit of patience from your end will also go a long way. If you don't see the results you want, it's time to break away from the manipulator so that you can begin new relationships that are balanced with mutual respect.

Putting Chapter 10 into Practice

Confidence is essential when communicating with a manipulator, and I'm not a fan of pretending to be confident when you're not, as a manipulator can see through it. Instead, practice what you want to say in advance. There are plenty of example phrases you can use, but you don't need to use them all at once. Your phrase should be short and concise. The more you talk, the more chances the manipulator has to convince you that you're wrong.

Exercise: The "Pause, Then Respond" Rule

When a manipulator tries to catch you off guard, pause for two seconds before saying anything. Use this time to think, *"Do I need to respond?"* or *"What's the simplest answer?"*

Example:

• Instead of explaining, say, "I'll think about it and let you know."

• Swap "sorry" for, "Thanks for letting me know."

• Or go with a simple, "Interesting point."

That pause keeps you in control. Manipulators crave quick reactions, so slowing down throws them off their game.

CHAPTER 11:
COMMUNICATION ≠ POWERLESSNESS

 Respond intelligently even to unintelligent treatment.

— *LAO TZU*

We are now aware that there will always be toxic people in our lives. Despite eliminating them as much as possible, new relationships might be started, and it won't be possible to avoid them completely.

You may start a new job you absolutely love—except for that one colleague. You may have a loved one who goes through a traumatic experience and starts to show toxic behavior. Learning how to speak to these people is your best tool for not only survival but also empowerment.

I, like many others, have gone through many different types of relationships that were completely unhealthy. One of two things tends to happen.

The unhealthy relationship drags on for much longer than it should, or it ends, often in a messy way. In both situations, there has been a significant breakdown in communication and the crucial conversations haven't taken place.

Why Communicate?

Talking about how we feel is incredibly hard, and it often seems easier to hold it all in, even remain angry at someone instead of telling them you have been hurt. The problem is that all the words that should be said weigh you down. We are reluctant to have these conversations because of fear or dread of reactions. Perhaps, deep down, we know the relationship is over, but discussing the problems will only confirm this. That alone can prevent us from communicating.

The irony is that speaking with difficult or toxic people can relieve many of the problems and make way for a healthier relationship. Because we tend to live in our own heads and don't rarely stop to consider how we are feeling, talking about them helps you to organize your mind and better describe emotions accurately. Once you rip the initial Band-Aid off and show your vulnerability, talking about how you feel can lead the way to deeper and more meaningful conversations for both of you. It's possible that the person you are dealing with is not toxic like we have seen. It could be that they are lacking in emotional awareness and genuinely don't understand the pain they cause you. In this case, opening up can be incredibly beneficial.

On the other hand, if it doesn't solve issues, you can end the relationship in a more respectful way without it dragging on unnecessarily. This necessary conversation can bring you closure. Closure is about understanding and accepting the end of a relationship. It could mean getting answers to your questions, understanding why things happened, and learning from your situation.

Many people struggle to move forward without closure. You may feel you want the abusive person to take some responsibility for what they have done, even an admission of guilt or an apology. This is where things get tricky, depending on the level of toxicity of the other person. You might get your closure, but toxic people will rarely hold themselves accountable.

Either way, learning how to speak to these types of people will take a great weight off your shoulders, free you from their toxic behavior, and enable you to regain your power. this is how you find closure without waiting for anything from the other person. By trusting your instincts and knowing what type of person you are dealing with, you can determine how much of yourself you are willing to reveal. That being said, if you know the person is toxic, your communication may need a different approach.

7 Tips for Communicating with a Toxic Person

1. Stay cold, show no emotion

We have discussed this in the context of dealing with manipulators and sociopaths, but it applies to all toxic people. While it sounds harsh, particularly if you enjoy being warm toward others, remember that you don't have to be cold with everyone, just with those who are difficult.

The problem is that regardless of their possible mental health issues, difficult people will use any hint of their emotions to manage and control the conversation. If you were to raise your voice even slightly, they could come back at you by saying you always get angry. If you defend yourself, you're considered defensive, and if you cry, you're labeled as too emotional.

You can be honest about your purpose for the conversation, and while facts are important, remain borderline cold.

2. Do not negotiate

The phrase "We do not negotiate with terrorists" has been used in everything from government policy to films and as a popular catchphrase for good reason! It's certainly a phrase that should be constantly playing in your mind. Imagine that this person is a terrorist, making unrealistic, dangerous demands and expecting you to succumb.

Let's face it: for a very long time, probably even years, you have been negotiating with toxic people, and it hasn't led you to a good place. During your conversations with difficult people, there is no gray area, no maybes, and no middle ground. There is black or white, yes or no, depending on your needs and what your instincts are telling you. Again, it sounds harsh and complicated, but you aren't crossing the line into being nasty—you are remaining firm.

3. Stand your ground, but don't be defensive

When our character or behavior is criticized, a natural response might be to become defensive. We feel the need to justify our actions or blame others for the problem. The most dangerous response is to stop listening to what they are saying, as it will cause a breakdown in communication.

Toxic people will go to any lengths to find your defensive button. They will bring up arguments or mistakes you made way back in the past, and they will highlight a weakness that they know will hurt you the most. They do all of this to get an emotional reaction from you.

You should always stand up for yourself and not let others drag up off-topic issues just to see you suffer. At the same time, make sure you are emotionally in control and also stay on topic. Assertively tell the person that you will not be disrespected.

4. Acknowledge that it'll never actually be your turn

It's not going to be your turn to be the one who makes logical sense, to speak without interruption, and to be right. You can keep fighting, or you can choose to accept this because it's the childish game they like to play.

You have the power to rise above this! If you think you will overpower them by beating them at their own game, you are only going to sink to their level. Keep your head held high and stay firm in your expression and values, as this is how they won't be able to drain your power.

5. Keep it short and sweet

Perhaps not short and sweet, as we are still aiming for the firm, non-emotional version of you.

Short and simple —definitely.

The longer you talk, the more likely you start speaking fluff and those emotions will get involved. More often than not, when you keep it short and simple, the conversation is also a lot less dramatic.

Know what point you want to make. Your part should include the problem and the solution. Don't worry if you come across as blunt. Blunt is not the same as rude or bad-mannered. This approach allows for things to be over faster.

6. Protect your Achilles' heel

We all have our weaknesses—not your quick temper or tendency to be overprotective of your kids. Your Achilles' heel here is that one vulnerability that hurts like a stab in the back. My ex would say, "You're mentally not right," and although it doesn't sound like a big deal, she knew it was a concern of mine, and she used it to throw me off balance in any argument.

Going forward and keeping your emotions out of conversations with difficult people will help you protect your weaknesses because they won't be able to see them. For those comfortable attacking your weak spots, prepare yourself in advance. You know that they will mention it, so have some breathing techniques or a happy place to go to in your mind instead of letting them get to you. It also helps to keep your goals in mind and remember why you are having the conversation in the first place.

7. Do it for yourself and not to win

We can all admit to having moments when there is an overwhelming urge to win an argument, even if you don't even know what winning looks like.

The truth is, nobody ever really wins an argument. As soon as either party sees it as something that can be won or lost, you have lost. Another good one is, "You may have won the battle, but you haven't won the war." The point of these conversations is to improve the relationship, not to win.

Conversations with difficult people are necessary for personal growth, a better life, more balance in a relationship, and many other more crucial reasons than scoring a point. Remember that you are doing this for yourself, and this should be your primary concern.

Exact Phrases to Use When Talking with Toxic People

Much of what we have looked at up to this point has been about mental preparation. It's now time to look at specific phrases you can use in your conversations with difficult people. My advice is never to use a phrase if it doesn't feel right for you. At the end of the day, these are all great ideas, but it will be up to you to decide which phrases are best to use in the conversation you are having at that time.

Rebeca Zung, attorney and author, created an excellent video about different types of phrases you can use with toxic people. Her YouTube video **"Phrases to Disarm a Narcissist"** will really help to inspire the right words for each situation. Let's look at some examples:

We know that difficult people are going to say things to get a rise. There is no truth behind these words, and the mental preparation we have worked on allows us to recognize them as empty and meaningless. To keep the situation calm, it's sometimes necessary to agree with difficult people. Since they will be looking for a reaction, these phrases will stop them in their tracks.

• I agree with you

• Okay, if that's how you feel

• You are right

You can only use these types of responses for things that don't matter to you. If somebody attacks your beliefs, religion, or values, then you shouldn't just agree. As much as you want to continue the conversation until they see your point of view, it's not going to happen.

So, it's best to end the conversation sooner rather than later:

• I don't agree, but we both have a right to our opinions

• We will have to agree to disagree

• Your opinion will feel right to you

Some situations will require "I" sentences, as you want the listener to pay attention to how you feel rather than how they make you feel. Other times, "we" is effective.

This way, you aren't blaming them but taking responsibility for your part in the situation:

• We need to improve our communication

• We have both made mistakes

• We can work on this together

You might also want to flatter their ego because, at the end of the day, this is what they require in a relationship. Getting them to weigh in and offer their opinion shows that you value what they have to say. This can also highlight just how ridiculous their idea or behavior is.

Still, don't use these phrases if you don't agree with the plan being put forward:

• What's your opinion on this?

• Do you think this is a good plan?

• How about if we try it this way?

Toxic people have low self-esteem, and there will be times when the best solution is to recognize this and try to help them boost their self-esteem. Rather than letting them feel ignored, show them that you are listening and that what they say matters to you.

• I hear what you are saying

• I understand where you are coming from

• I respect that (and repeat the comment)

Adapt these phrases for your particular situation or the person you are dealing with. Don't forget to practice saying them aloud so that they sound natural and not forced.

Preparing Your Thick Skin for the Harsh Words They Will Use

It amazes me that in English, as well as most other languages, there are more negative words than positive. There are seven basic emotions that are recognized in most cultures: joy, fear, anger, sadness, disgust, shame, and guilt. How many do you see that are positive? It's no wonder society finds it easier to be negative than positive.

Verbal abuse is a very real thing, and the hurtful words toxic people use can have long-lasting effects. As we can't control what other people say, we can only learn to protect ourselves from this. Negative contractions like "You can't…" and "You don't…" are two obvious examples that don't appear to be that bad. However, after months or years of being told you can't do something, you start to believe it. Here are some other words that you need to prepare for so you can protect yourself:

• Dumb/stupid/fool

• Irresponsible/thoughtless/careless

• You're a failure/you're no good

• Ashamed/embarrassed by you

• You're a disappointment

• Weird/strange

• Mad/crazy/wrong in the head

• Boring/grumpy/antisocial

• Lazy/useless/inferior

• Ugly/fat/scruffy

• Arrogant/bossy

• The word "hate"

Decide now how you will respond to each of these words. If someone calls you lazy and you know it's not true, you might want to agree and ignore it. If a word hurts your feelings, like calling you ugly, you know this isn't true, but it's not fair that you should tolerate it, so stand up for yourself.

Master Your Conversation Skills

Anybody can talk, but not everyone has taken the time to master conversation skills. This is a vital skill not just for toxic people but for life. As you start to free yourself from difficult people, you will start to create new relationships. The following conversation skills from experts will help you be the master of conversations with all types of people.

1. Really listen

We can all confess to a moment when someone was talking, and we were preoccupied with thoughts about what to eat for dinner. Listening is essential so that you can respond appropriately. Not listening leads to miscommunication and frustration.

2. Don't judge others

Everybody has their own story, their own sufferings, and their own reasons. Don't make judgments about others because we rarely know the whole story. Just as we don't like people making judgments about us, it's only fair to act the same way.

3. Be observant

It's amazing how many ways there are to start a conversation just by being observant. When you pay attention to what people wear, logos, or even colors, you can strike up a new conversation. For example, I once saw two women with travel mugs that said, "Seriously." It didn't make sense to me, but as soon as they noticed, a great *Grey's Anatomy* debate began.

4. Silence is okay

Don't feel the need to force a conversation just because you fear silence. It's perfectly normal to have breaks in a conversation, giving people a chance to focus their thoughts.

5. Have interesting things to say

On the other hand, watch out for that awkward silence! Awkward silence often occurs because people have run out of things to say. To prevent this, try keeping up-to-date on the latest news, but save the information for when the conversation runs dry. Be aware of your audience, especially when it comes to topics like religion and politics.

6. Ask for opinions

Asking for other people's opinions can give them a real confidence boost. People like to know that their opinions are valued. You can ask about restaurants, books, and TV. One word of advice, don't ask for an opinion if you aren't going to like the answer, and remember that it's alright if you don't agree.

7. Take care with humor

Humor is like conversation topics; you have to know your audience. Not everyone will share the same sense of humor, more so across different cultures. That being said, humor is a great ice-breaker, and you should feel comfortable using it. Look for some clean, politically correct jokes or stories that will please the crowd.

8. Expand your answers

One-word answers can come across as a little rude. If someone asks you a question or your opinion, expand your answer so that the conversation can be taken further.

9. Avoid question bombardment

Asking some questions can show a genuine interest in the other person. Question bombardment could make them feel like they are in an interview, and if you aren't careful, cross their boundary. As a general rule, ask questions that you would be comfortable answering.

10. Recognize the signs that the conversation is over

There is a little old lady at the end of my road, and I always take time to chat with her, but she will go on—to the extent that I am in my car and she is still talking. If you aren't capable of knowing when to end a conversation, people may be reluctant to start one with you.

Because the way we deal with difficult people will vary from relationship to relationship, we need to take a closer look at specific methods to handle parents, partners, and friends. In the next chapter, we will look at practical solutions to deal with the difficult loved ones in our lives.

Putting Chapter 11 into Practice

Don't make the mistake of pushing yourself out of your comfort zone and using phrases you wouldn't feel comfortable saying. Review this chapter and choose some powerful sentences or combine ideas to create new ones you would feel confident saying.

CHAPTER 12: DEALING WITH DIFFICULT PEOPLE

 Peace is not the absence of conflict, it is the ability to handle conflict by peaceful means.

— *RONALD REAGAN*

In this chapter, we'll adapt the techniques from Chapter 10 for dealing with friends, partners, and family members. To recap on dealing with difficult people in general, remember to choose the right phrases for each situation. We'll look into more options for each circumstance.

Whether you're dealing with an impossible client, your overbearing parents, or your controlling partner, you'll have to think about those hurtful words they might use and prepare yourself. One of the biggest tips for dealing with difficult people is to avoid revealing your emotions, as they know just what words to use to get you to react.

Finally, becoming a master of conversation skills is going to improve relationships, particularly new ones. Your conversation skills are crucial for your personal and professional life and will increase your confidence. Keep in mind that these techniques may not always work on certain personality types. For this reason, we'll cover various personality types and the people you interact with regularly.

Powerful Phrases for Dealing with Challenging Personalities

Challenging personalities include those we have talked about, such as narcissists and manipulators, and these types of people require a special kind of treatment. If you're dealing with the most challenging types of personalities but they are making an effort to improve their behavior, these phrases may also help.

It can also be the drama queens in our lives, the suffocators, the pessimists, and the controllers. Each of these challenging personalities can appear in any area of your life. We will start with some useful phrases that can be used in a multitude of situations:

• I understand that you didn't do it on purpose, however...

• I apologize if I didn't explain myself well.

• I'm sorry that you misunderstood me.

• I do see your point of view.

• I appreciate your opinion.

• I think that we should talk about this more.

• Perhaps we can find a time to talk about a compromise.

• What do you think about this idea?

• How would you feel if we did X instead of Y?

• Let's look at the facts and keep opinions to one side for a bit.

• I respect that we see things differently, but we need to find a way to overcome this.

• I want to come up with a solution with you without interrupting each other.

• I'm glad we talked. Is there anything else you want to say?

As with the phrases we have seen before and subsequent phrases, stick to the ones that you feel comfortable with because you need to sound assertive, confident, and natural. If a phrase like "Perhaps we can find a time to talk about a compromise" is over the top for you or the person you are talking to, you could rephrase it to "Maybe we can chat and find a middle ground."

6 Steps to Effective Conflict Resolution and What Not to Do

Conflict can be both a verb and a noun. As a verb, it means to be incompatible or have differences in opinions. As a noun, it refers to a dispute or an argument. We can't shy away from conflicts or avoid them.

It's healthier to handle the conflict at the moment so that the situation doesn't escalate. Like communication skills, conflict resolution is a valuable life skill to master. To resolve conflicts, you can follow these six simple steps:

1. Put the brakes on and think

It all comes back to emotions. Someone may have said or done something that caused you pain and to feel upset. Our minds will naturally jump to the person and not the situation, and when you focus on the person, emotions have a habit of taking control over your logical side. This closes our minds and prevents us from being objective. Always pause before you speak so that you remain calm.

2. Expand your perspective

As we mature, we become better at evaluating situations from different perspectives. Putting ourselves in other peoples' shoes is a great way to get a better understanding of what is really happening and to try to see how the other person is feeling.

A great pro tip here is to play devil's advocate with yourself — disagree with your own opinion to come up with other ways of looking at the situation. Doing this might show you that, in the end, there may not even be a conflict. And if there is, you will be better equipped to handle it.

3. Agree on the problem

Next, it is time for both or all parties to define the problem. Until everyone agrees on the problem, it will be impossible for perspectives and solutions to be shared. Everyone needs to have the opportunity to agree or disagree on the definition of the issue without getting carried away with their opinions.

4. Share perspectives

The key here is to let everyone share their opinions and show they are being heard. Interrupting, checking your phone, or generally being distant is a sure way to aggravate others. Only when everyone is listening carefully to each idea you will be able to move on to solutions.

5. Respect each other's solutions

Much like the perspectives, people need to be given the chance to express their ideas to resolve the conflict. Going back to our basic human rights, everyone has the right to their opinion, and therefore, each must be respected. After solutions have been discussed, you can then look at the potential for compromise.

6. Agree on the final solution

Once everyone has been a little flexible, a solution to keep everyone happy can be reached. It's worth emphasizing the solution and ensuring that the person or people understand and have said all they feel they have to. End the conversation on a positive note, such as, "I'm really happy we worked this out, and I know we can do it again if necessary." (Everson, 2014)

Aside from what you should do, there are also a few things that you shouldn't do when trying to resolve conflicts:

• Avoid using extreme adverbs of frequency like always and never. They may come across as exaggerating and blowing things out of proportion.

• Don't stew on matters. The longer you think about something, the bigger it is likely to become, and then it becomes easier to drag irrelevant matters into the conflict.

• Pick a time that also suits the other parties. We often talk about choosing a time when you are calm, but it's only fair that you ask someone if you can have a few minutes when they are free to ensure they are in the right frame of mind too.

• Don't assume anything. When you assume you have understood everything or you assume that they have, there is a great possibility that everyone walks away thinking a problem has been solved when it hasn't.

Dealing with Difficult Parents

Take a moment to think about how you view your parents. I know this changes as we grow up, even more so when you have your own children. However, we tend to forget that our parents are actually only humans, just as we are. We set high expectations for them because, after all, they should know better. Aren't they always telling us this?

When you take away the parent element, they are subject to the same emotions, struggles, and conflicts that we are. The difference is that they have to live with the fear of their mistakes being judged by their children. The first step in dealing with difficult parents is to remember that they are human and to lower your expectations. If you know that a sociopathic friend isn't going to change, why would you expect a sociopathic parent to?

When it comes to our parents, one of the most common manipulative techniques they use is the guilt trip. They will likely ask you to do something, and when you say no, there will be some pushback. When you stand your ground, the big guns come out. You might have to put up with phrases like "It's okay! It's not like I raised you for over 18 years," or "Your cousin would never put your aunt in a home."

The most blindingly obvious are "You owe me" and "If you love me…" and yet we still fall for them. You need to put a stop to this emotional manipulation. They love you, you love them, and nobody needs to prove that. What you should do is tell them you know what they are trying to do and that it will no longer work.

If you're still looking for your parent's approval, it's time to overcome this. Parents often don't approve of the decisions their adult child makes; you may even feel like they are trying to relive their life through yours. They may withhold approval as a form of punishment or simply because they are unable to support their children because of a lack of emotions. As soon as you stop looking for your parents' approval, your dealings with them will become simpler, and asserting yourself will get easier.

On that note, be assertive with difficult parents. It's not rude or disrespectful because you can still be polite, even caring. At the same time, you can be honest and use "I" statements to express your feelings. Let go of any assumptions; they may listen, they may not. The point is that you stop allowing them to control your life— empower yourself and decide on the level of contact you are comfortable with.

Power Phrases to Deal with Difficult Parents

• I'll always respect you, but I have thought about this carefully.

• I feel suffocated when you won't give me space.

• It's great that you want to help me at home, but there should be limits.

• I know you're frustrated, but you can't take that out on me.

• I can't make plans this weekend, but I would like to do something next weekend.

• I will not tolerate you insulting me.

• If you keep crossing the line, I won't come over for dinner.

• It's fine if you don't agree with my opinions, but you do need to respect them.

Tips for Confronting Partners

Just because your partner is difficult doesn't mean the relationship is doomed. There are still reasons why you fell in love and plenty to look forward to once you have learned how best to deal with them while guarding your own happiness. This starts with being very clear about what your reality is, understanding your emotions, and realizing your boundaries.

Being clear on these matters will stop you from playing into their reality, allowing them to make you feel as if they are always the victim. Understanding your emotions better can help you avoid getting sucked into the same type of behavior. Your emotional intelligence will keep you on the right path so you don't join in with their negativity.

Take some time to talk to your partner about their feelings. They may have some bottled-up emotions that are causing their toxic behavior. While you are being compassionate, you have to remember that it's not your place to fix them. They have to want to do this! The conversation also has to be balanced, so you should also have the chance to talk about your feelings. As soon as your partner starts to raise voice, become aggressive, or you feel threatened in any way, it's time to walk away—at least for long enough to calm down.

You must resolve the conflict with a difficult partner. Don't just assume that the issue has been resolved now that you are both calm. Burying it only means that it may resurface in the next conflict.

You're going to need the thickest skin possible for difficult partners. We open our hearts up to them, we trust them, and it's incredibly painful when partners use words to break our spirits. I like to imagine it as a mental game of tennis, with every insult or lie being the balls, and my mind is the tennis racket hitting them away from me. You can also practice deep breathing to help the words flow away from you. Do not take this personally, and remember that it is not your fault.

Power Phrases to Deal with Difficult Partners

• I know we have both had a long day, but let's find time later to talk.

• I love that you want to spend time with your parents, but I need to spend time with mine too.

• If you are going to be home late, please let me know. That way I won't have to worry.

• You can choose between the laundry or vacuuming. Which do you prefer?

• I don't appreciate it when you disrespect my authority in front of the children.

• I have asked you not to raise your voice. If you continue, I will leave.

• I am here for you, and I want to help, but we have to be in this together.

• I want to see your point of view, but I can't when you're angry and shouting.

Handling Tough Talks with Friends

The first thing to consider is what type of friend you are dealing with. Friends of friends and acquaintances who are toxic, you should just walk away from. Life is too short to let these types of people impact your life. Our tips will help with any depth of friendship, but consider which friends deserve your energy.

The best thing about friendships is that there usually isn't such a close tie as there is with your partner or parents because you aren't living with them. It doesn't mean the relationship isn't just as important; it's like the middle path. More often than not, you have known them for years, even longer than your partner, but they know you differently from your parents. Friends are a great place to start practicing communication skills and setting boundaries.

Like with all conflicts, you need to begin by understanding how you feel and the cause of your unhappiness. Know what you want to say and practice it a few times, preferably in the mirror so you can see your body language. You need to check that your shoulders are straight and that you aren't hunched over. Your arms and legs shouldn't be crossed so that you appear open. Don't forget to smile! As well as coming across as confident, you want to seem approachable.

Call your friend to arrange a time and place that is convenient for both of you. This place should be free from distractions, so make it a coffee shop but not your usual spot. It's important that you meet rather than try to deal with the problem via text or call because it's easy to misunderstand each other.

Use the sandwich technique: start with something kind and positive, then address the issue directly. Your friend needs to understand the root of the problem and how it makes you feel, but they don't need to see you getting emotional. Getting angry will only make matters worse. Encourage your friend to respond with their perspective and feelings and pay attention! Finish your "sandwich" by ending on positives, making new plans, or talking about the good parts of your friendship.

Power Phrases to Deal with Difficult Friends

• I'm sorry if this seems insignificant to you, but…

• I love that I can speak honestly with you.

• I feel like you ignore me when I try to talk about my situation.

• I need some time before I make a decision.

• I have so much fun with you, but I get upset when…

• I know that you're angry, but shouting isn't going to help.

• It hurts when you laugh at my flaws.

• I see where you are coming from; however, I would like it if you could understand my point of view.

Tackling Family Conflicts

Family members who aren't parents are a little bit like friends. The conflicts that arise are still going to cause you stress, but it's somewhat easier to limit your contact and even break ties if necessary. It's always worth trying one more time to get the relationship back on track with the new knowledge you have. Begin by deciding if this difficult family member is caring and doing it in the wrong way or if they are just pure toxic. If you feel that they are toxic and manipulative, then follow the techniques we looked at before. If it's a family member trying to control you, smother you, or treat you in ways that hurt you or make you feel uncomfortable, it's time to work on strengthening your boundaries.

You may have already tried to establish your boundaries with family members, but it's possible that they didn't take you seriously. It might also mean that you weren't sure about your boundaries yourself, which is why others are crossing them. If you firmly believe that you know what your boundaries are and you have expressed them clearly, you now know that your consequences aren't in place.

One tip that works really well is to listen to family members as if it's the first time. After so many years of hearing the same thing, we tend to tune out the same nagging and complaining, and we start to switch off. Remember that even though they have said the same thing numerous times, you should listen like it's the first time because you are a different person now. You are mentally stronger, you are calm and in control of your emotions, and you will listen with a new perspective and new insights on how to handle the situation (www.harleytherapy.co.uk).

Power Phrases to Deal with Family Members

• I respect that you have more experience, but I am going to do things my way.

- I have explained before that I don't like it when you show up unannounced.

- When I say no, it's to the activity, not to you.

- I need some time to myself this weekend, but I can help you during the week.

- I need you to understand that if you insist on insulting me, I won't join in with your plans.

- If you are upset about something, I am here for you, but I won't listen if you are going to shout.

- My intention isn't to hurt you, but I don't intend to walk on eggshells.

- I am hurt by your nasty words, and I'm offering you a chance to talk about what is bothering you.

Tips for Confronting Difficult Colleagues

We often try to take on the attitude of walking out of the office and leaving work behind. If we are honest with ourselves, what goes on during those eight hours at work has a habit of following us and even impacting our personal relationships. I'm sure I'm not the only one who has experienced a colleague behaving in a toxic way at work, and then I go home and take it out on a loved one.

You may have dedicated years to your career, you have to put yourself first. Isn't it only fair that you put your career, your responsibilities, and your reputation first? Toxic colleagues will do anything to make you look bad so that they either look better or you feel bad about yourself. The end goal is to advance their own career.

As soon as you spot difficult people in your workplace, you have to put a stop to it right away before it escalates. Even if the behavior seems trivial—taking your stapler, for example—it could be the start of something more troublesome.

The most professional method of dealing with difficult colleagues is to strictly follow the six steps we mentioned earlier. So, stop and think, expand your perspectives, agree on the problem, and share perspectives. Respect the ideas that people put forward and agree on the final solution, remembering that some compromise will have to be made.

Timing is even more crucial when dealing with difficult colleagues. Although you have outstanding communication skills, your colleague may not. To avoid making a scene, you shouldn't call people out on their behavior, for example, in the middle of a meeting.

One thing that won't do you any favors is gossiping about the problem to others. Unfortunately, you are using toxic behavior to try and beat toxic behavior. If you need to communicate issues with management, do so in an informative way rather than gossiping. Take time to prepare what you need to say without any fluff.

Regardless of who you are dealing with, people are busy and don't need lengthy discussions for something that could be dealt with in five minutes. If you are doing it by email, reread the email before hitting send to ensure everything is included in one go to prevent frustration for the reader if a second email is needed.

You may have heard that in relationships, you should never go to bed angry with each other. Try to follow the same motto at work. Be the bigger person, and at the end of the day, let them know that it was great to clear the air or thank them for listening. Aim for both of you to go home as if the situation is resolved.

Don't forget to keep records of everything, especially when things start impacting other staff members. If you have a conversation with someone, following up with an email recapping the key points is a good idea.

This is a good way to double-check that you are both on the same page, but you should also have a digital copy in case your integrity is questioned later down the line.

Power Phrases to Deal with Colleagues

• I want to talk to you about a matter impacting the whole team.

• It bothers me when you criticize me in front of others.

• I don't find that kind of humor suitable for the office.

• I understand you might be comfortable bending the rules, but it's not fair to the others.

• Please avoid sending non-work-related messages and emails, as I'm too busy to read all of them.

• I like my colleagues, and I don't want to hear unkind things about them.

• I will not tolerate backstabbing and mind games in order to advance your career.

• I know you are very smart and experienced, but I also have valuable opinions that I would like you to consider.

Troubleshooting: Putting the Techniques into Context

Let's take a look at three different situations and how we could effectively resolve conflicts, even though efforts have been made before.

Laura suspects her partner, Anthony, is withdrawing emotionally. He often comes home late, citing work obligations, and their once vibrant conversations have dwindled to mundane exchanges. Feeling neglected, Laura's mind races to the conclusion that he might be involved with someone else. Rather than addressing her concerns directly, she starts suggesting activities to reconnect, which only makes her seem clingy and further alienates Anthony. As a result, Laura becomes more anxious and frustrated.

To address this situation effectively, Laura should first consider various perspectives, including the worst-case scenario. Instead of fixating on the possibility of infidelity, she should think practically about what separation would mean for her life. Preparing for a constructive conversation is crucial, so she should find an appropriate time to talk, ideally when both are relaxed. It's important that this conversation doesn't feel threatening or dramatic.

In the meantime, Laura can organize her thoughts using phrases like:

• "I've been feeling a bit disconnected lately, and I'd like to understand what's going on between us."

• "I realize I might not have communicated my feelings well, but I hope we can share our perspectives."

• "I appreciate how hard you're working, but I feel our relationship needs attention too."

• "I'd like to hear about what's been stressing you out so I can better support you."

There's a possibility that Anthony might respond by saying he feels overwhelmed with work and hasn't known how to share that with her. Conversely, he could express that he's feeling emotionally distant due to personal issues unrelated to their relationship.By jumping to conclusions and trying to read Anthony's mind, Laura has made a common mistake: assuming the worst without fully understanding his perspective. A healthy conversation, rooted in openness and curiosity, can help clear misunderstandings and strengthen their bond.

Jimmy is fed up with his loud-mouthed colleague who belittles everyone but then sucks up to management. He's like a real Jekyll and Hyde, and you never know which side of him you're going to see. Jimmy has made sarcastic cracks about his coworkers' behavior, but any criticisms are like water off a duck's back. As the boss starts to show favoritism toward the brownnoser, the tension in the office starts to rise. This colleague has no interest in rectifying his behavior because he has a strict timeline for his career advancement.

Sarcastic and even direct comments have no effect, so Jimmy has to find ways to make sure that tasks and responsibilities remain fair in the office so that even though the behavior may frustrate people, it won't affect the team's productivity. Obviously, there is little point in speaking to the boss as the colleague has manipulated how the boss views things. Jimmy comes up with a plan to introduce project management software and speaks to team members who are also looking to resolve this behavior. Using project management software, every team member is delegated tasks and deadlines, and it's easy to see who is doing what and when. The boss gets a complete overview, and there is a digital copy of tasks and communications.

Lisa has always enjoyed a close relationship with her brother, Mark. They share many interests and often hang out together. However, Mark has started making offhand comments about Lisa's career choices and personal life, which she initially brushed off as jokes. Over time, these remarks have become increasingly hurtful, leading to tension in their family gatherings.

After several uncomfortable moments, Lisa decides it's time to talk to Mark about how his comments affect her. When she first approaches him, he dismisses her feelings, claiming she's just being overly sensitive. This reaction leaves Lisa feeling frustrated and questioning whether she's overreacting. To prepare for a deeper conversation, Lisa reflects on their past interactions and realizes that Mark's comments have been consistent and unwelcome. She decides to approach him again, this time focusing on her feelings rather than accusations.

During their conversation, Lisa uses "I" statements to communicate her feelings: "I feel hurt when you make jokes about my job. It makes me doubt my choices." She also asks Mark if anything is going on in his life that might be causing him to act this way, opening the door for a more honest discussion.

Finally, Lisa sets a clear boundary: "I'm okay with light teasing, but if your comments continue to hurt me, I'll need to limit our time together." This way, Lisa not only protects her feelings but also encourages Mark to reflect on his behavior and consider the impact it has on their relationship.

With the majority of difficult people, these techniques will get to the bottom of the problems and allow you to move forward, with the option to readdress issues in the future if need be. It's up to you to decide whether these people are making efforts to improve their behavior or not. If some time passes and you see the same behaviors repeated, or your levels of stress have not improved, it's time to consider creating distance between you or breaking contact completely. I know we are always hopeful that people will change, but it's essential to remember that the emotional strains you feel won't just disappear overnight. The longer the conflict goes on, the harder it can be to overcome in the long run.

Putting Chapter 12 into Practice

Think about some conflicts you have had in the past, preferably within different types of relationships such as romantic, work, and family. With the information you now have from this chapter, how would you have handled these conflicts? What would you have said for each response the other person gave you?

Oh, But Wait—There's More!

To support you as you master these strategies, here are some **Extra Bonuses** to keep you steady when things get messy:

✓ ***Bonus 1:*** *Shut Down Toxic Talk – Smart Scripts for Sticky Situations.*

✓ ***Bonus 2:*** *How to Deal with a Toxic Person: Practical Workbook.*

To get your extra materials, just scan the QR code. Think of it as your all-access pass to handling the tough situations with style! Because let's be real – practice makes progress.

CHAPTER 13: EMOTIONAL ABUSE: YOUR GUIDE

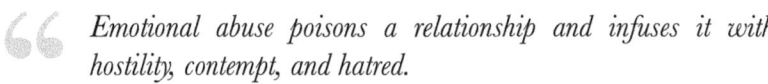 *Emotional abuse poisons a relationship and infuses it with hostility, contempt, and hatred.*

— *BEVERLY ENGEL*

Our focus up to now has been on techniques and strategies for the difficult and toxic people in our lives. This is only the first half of taking back control of your life and becoming happy.

The impact these people leave on you doesn't just disappear because you have mastered how to handle them. There are both long-term and short-term effects of emotional abuse that need to be addressed.

This chapter marks the beginning of focusing on you to emotionally cleanse yourself and be ready for a fresh start.

It's possible you might not even be aware of the damage caused by this toxic behavior. Emotional abuse isn't like physical abuse. There are no cuts and scars to see.

Awareness of emotional abuse is essential so that you can focus your energy in the right direction for a positive change.

The Short-Term Side Effects of Emotional Abuse

Initially, you might be completely taken aback by your loved one's behavior, especially if something has happened out of the blue. You might feel shocked and confused. Male or female, you may find yourself crying frequently. It's important to be careful that this doesn't have a knock-on effect on your sleep. A lack of sleep can quickly become a physical problem and make it harder to take care of your emotional needs.

It's perfectly normal to feel anxious or even scared about not knowing what sort of behavior is going to come next. If the anxiety isn't controlled, it may turn into panic attacks, again a physical reaction to fear or anxiety. Signs of a panic attack include sweating, chills or hot flashes, dizziness or trembling, heart palpitations, and hyperventilation.

Short-term side effects of emotional abuse can go from one extreme to another. You might find yourself becoming aggressive (a defense mechanism after abuse), or you can end up feeling completely helpless as if you can't do anything right. Your confidence may be so shattered that you avoid eye contact or become more passive than usual.

Some people will feel a mixture of hopelessness and powerlessness. Though similar, they aren't the same. Being powerless means you aren't able to change a situation while being hopeless means losing all hope for change.

While unfounded, people who have been abused often feel guilty, as if it's their own fault. Or it's possible to feel shame and humiliation, questioning why you "let" the abuse happen, although your logical mind will tell you that you didn't let anything happen as the behavior is the responsibility of the other person.

Finally, in the short term, you may struggle with feelings of loneliness. If it's a partner, assuming you will remain alone for the rest of your life is common. If the abuser is a friend, you may also start to question your other friendships. Not surprisingly, abused people can feel unloved and unattractive.

You have probably taught yourself how to put on a brave face, to push those emotions down so that others around you can't see your suffering. Eventually, though, you won't be able to hide the emotional toll of abuse, nor should you. On the one hand, it's not fair to you. On the other hand, there are still people in your life who care about you and don't want to see you suffering in this way.

The strain of emotional abuse can lead to moodiness. I know from my own experiences that this only makes you feel worse because now you have the guilt of snapping at others who might not have done anything wrong. Aside from anxiety causing you to miss out on that all-important sleep, you might find yourself having bad dreams, even nightmares.

Because of the lack of sleep and the emotional strain you are under, it won't be long before you find it difficult to concentrate. No matter how hard you try to focus on, for example, work, your mind will shoot back to the problems you have been through.

Some people will suffer from headaches or muscle tension, particularly across the neck and shoulders. It's almost as if you can feel the emotional abuse building up in your muscles.

And, yes, these aches and pains may also affect your sleep.

The Long-Term Side Effects of Emotional Abuse

If left unresolved, the short-term side effects won't just disappear. It's more probable that they will escalate into something more serious. All of the short-term side effects can quickly manifest into heightened anxiety and/or depression. Sleep disturbances can lead to further emotional instability and also contribute to the lack of energy you may be experiencing. The first waves of low self-esteem can develop into more serious problems such as social anxiety and withdrawal. Difficulties in concentration can become more severe and impact your ability to remember things and make the right decisions.

Watch out for denial. This is a good one because so many people fail to understand the depression spectrum. You might experience a profound sense of sadness or emptiness and deny the fact that it could be depression. While many imagine depression as great bouts of heavy, pessimistic thoughts and feelings, there are various types, ranging from constant sadness to thoughts of suicide or attempted suicide. Let's take a quick look at some of the most common types of depression:

Major depression: Also referred to as clinical depression and is characterized by experiencing symptoms mentioned above for the majority of the time and on most days.

Persistent depressive disorder: A depression that lasts for two or more years is defined as persistent, which can also be broken down into dysthymia (low-grade persistent depression) or chronic major depression.

Manic depression: The preferred term today is bipolar disorder, but it involves feeling extremely energetic and positive one minute and then experiencing low moments of major depression.

Seasonal affective disorder: Appropriately abbreviated to SAD, this type of major depression occurs during months that have less light.

Psychotic depression: When the symptoms of major depression are accompanied by psychotic symptoms like hallucinations, delusions, and paranoia.

Postpartum depression: Postpartum depression is often related to giving birth, but that's not to say that toxic relationships won't contribute. It's also important to recognize that this is not just a type of depression that women suffer from. Approximately 1 in 10 men experience postpartum depression in the weeks and months after the arrival of a baby (WebMD, 2020).

Situational depression: Also known as stress response syndrome, certain major events in our lives can cause large amounts of stress and depression.

Atypical depression: As the name implies, this is not the typical depression of constant sadness or feeling low. Your mood will improve with positive things that occur in life, though this burst of happiness isn't permanent.

Regardless of the severity of your depression, you must visit your doctor. There are so many types of therapies available today, not just antidepressants. You aren't going to just "shake it off" or get over it, and the last thing you want to do is ignore depression so that it gets to the point where you consider ending your own life. Speaking from the heart, it is never as bad as you think as long as you are open to getting some help, and there is no shame in getting this help. It's almost impossible to see the silver lining right now, but it will only get better from here on because you have chosen it to be this way.

Traumatic events and stress can both lead to insomnia. To be diagnosed with a sleep disorder, insomniacs will have sleep difficulties for a minimum of three nights a week for three months. These sleep difficulties can be related to falling asleep, staying asleep, or both. It's estimated that one-third of adults show symptoms of insomnia, and 6-10% meet the criteria for insomnia disorder (American Psychiatric Association, 2013). Insomnia is very much linked to mood swings and irritability, and it's going to impact your ability to concentrate.

We all experience some unexplainable pain every now and again, and because it's physical, we don't relate it to the emotional abuse that we have been through. The nervous system keeps sending pain signals even though there is no reason for them. This can sometimes be in the same area as an old injury that healed a long time ago, or it could be completely random. Research shows that there is a connection between trauma and chronic pain. There is a theory behind this: the body has been so used to a heightened stress response because of the dangerous or toxic environment, and the response to the stress becomes abnormal and manifests into pain.

There are also many links between the long-term effects of emotional abuse. Chronic pain can be linked to depression, insomnia impacts concentration, and that overall feeling as if you have no energy or motivation. Both insomnia and chronic pain have connections to post-traumatic stress disorder (PTSD). Children who were exposed to abuse and went on to suffer from PTSD showed worse pain-related functioning and the ability to manage routine tasks. Between 60-90% of people with PTSD also suffer from insomnia (Ohayan, 2000). Those with PTSD are also more likely to attempt suicide, with one study showing around 27% of sufferers having attempted suicide at some point in their lives (Ramsawh, Fullerton, Mash, 2014).

The final long-term effect of emotional abuse is social withdrawal. Human beings are social creatures—pack animals, so to speak. We need social interactions to improve our mood, increase brain health, and boost our sense of security. When our emotional self has taken a severe beating, so do our confidence and self-esteem. You might find that you are no longer keen on doing your old hobbies and activities, closing yourself off from people.

The lack of energy discourages you from going out with friends, and overall, you are not comfortable in social situations. It might seem safer to stay away from people to prevent getting hurt again. However, the opposite will happen. We should distance ourselves from those who are toxic and surround ourselves with positive, supportive people to build up our strength and benefit from social interactions.

Both short- and long-term side effects are interconnected and may not neatly fit into specific categories. Many of the symptoms will be linked. You may experience only one or two symptoms or any number of them at once. In the next chapter, we will look into the different ways you can begin the healing process from emotional abuse.

Misconceptions About Emotional Abuse

Myths and misconceptions are extremely dangerous. They can make people think that emotional abuse is limited to a certain type of person or isn't as bad as other types of abuse. When you think of emotional abuse, it's easy to imagine a female being abused by her partner. With this misconception, people don't see emotional abuse in other situations. Though women are more likely to suffer emotional abuse, it's something that occurs in all types of relationships and all genders.

Without understanding the cycle of abuse, people think that the abused don't want to do anything about it, or worse, they actually like it. Breaking free from emotional abuse is complex, and myths about it can diminish the effects and question the severity of the abuse. These misconceptions take away accountability, letting the abuser get away with their behavior.

Another myth is that some behaviors with emotional abuse are attractive or affectionate. Some confuse controlling with BDSM (Bondage and Discipline/Domination and Submission and Sadism and Masochism), which only confuses our understanding of the culture. BDSM requires respect and above all, consent—abuse doesn't (National Network to End Domestic Violence, 2016). Constant calling and texting or needing to spend excessive time with someone isn't a sign of love, it's a lack of trust and an attempt at controlling another person.

It's essential that myths and misconceptions about emotional abuse are addressed so that behaviors don't continue to be normalized. Don't be scared to correct others who are confused about emotional abuse.

From Their Eyes

This is by no means a justification for abusive behavior, nor does it give them an excuse for the way they treat you. This moment to take perspective can help you understand more about your own experiences. There are various reasons why a person becomes abusive, and it might not be because they have a mental or personality disorder. It's possible that emotional abuse is caused by their own childhood and witnessing emotional abuse as normal. There could be a lot of pent-up anger, and they can't control it.

In some cases, the abuser may have issues with their own emotions. Aside from a lack of empathy, they might be afraid, and this fear could be fueling their need for control. Their emotional abuse may be a defense mechanism. It's as if they feel they have been backed into a corner, and the only way involves being abusive—again, not your fault. A lack of boundaries is another potential reason. Your abuser sadly may not understand your limits because they can't see you as a separate entity. It's hard for them to understand that you have the right to space and other boundaries.

I can't stress enough that this is not an excuse for abusive behavior, but they might just be at the end of their tether. Stress and exhaustion build up, and they lash out when they can't take any more. Nevertheless, we can all go through times like this. The difference is that the abuser doesn't have healthy coping strategies.

Finally, there are times when the abused becomes the abuser, known as reactive abuse. When someone is abused, emotionally or physically, their fight-or-flight response kicks in, and as a defense mechanism, they become abusive to protect themselves.

Paul had been in an abusive relationship where his girlfriend constantly made him feel worthless. He was never right, his opinions were belittled, and nothing he did was good enough compared to his girlfriend's ex. Eventually, Paul ended up shouting at his girlfriend and even aggressively punching tables and walls, which was completely against his character.

In the case of reactive abuse, it's not entirely the fault of the person, and you may even find that you have also started reacting to emotional abuse. It's necessary to take a step back, accept responsibility, and make changes. This could mean discovering your own coping mechanisms as well as overcoming your emotional abuse.

I know I'm repeating myself, but it's that important—if you have any concerns, don't hesitate to contact a medical professional. Nothing is too trivial, and with such a wide range of support available today, the benefits of taking better care of yourself and seeking professional help will speed up your healing process and make sure you stay on the right track.

Putting Chapter 13 into Practice

Spend some time tracking symptoms of emotional abuse. Notice how the abuse makes you feel, not just in the moment but also afterward. Jot down moments when you felt dismissed or drained after an interaction—what was said, how you felt, and how it affected the rest of your day or other relationships. Before you can start to heal, you need to understand exactly what needs to be healed!

Exercise: The "Three Strikes" Rule

Some people love to test your limits, but here's a simple policy to keep things clear: the "Three Strikes" rule. Each time this person behaves in a way that's dismissive, manipulative, or downright rude, give them a mental "strike."

After three strikes, make a conscious decision to shift the way you interact—whether that means setting tighter boundaries, reducing contact, or just treating them as a fascinating case study in what *not* to put up with. This rule isn't about punishing them—it's about protecting you.

CHAPTER 14: HEALING FROM EMOTIONAL ABUSE

 Healing doesn't mean the damage never existed. It means the damage no longer controls our lives.

— AKSHAY DUBEY

This chapter will be short but highly influential. We have carefully looked at the impacts of emotional abuse and have compiled 20 tips on how to overcome these side effects as you start to put more and more distance between you and your toxic environment:

1. Acknowledge the abuse

The negative emotions connected with abuse can often lead us into a state of denial, shame, and even humiliation. Because of this, it's easier to ignore the symptoms of abuse rather than admit they are occurring. If you don't recognize that it's broken, you won't be able to start fixing it—or, in this case, healing.

2. Define a healthy relationship

If you have been trapped in an unhealthy relationship for a long time, it's hard to see clearly what constitutes a healthy one. Whether it's a partner, friend, or family member, you should be able to say no without feeling bad, express your needs and feelings openly, and be able to resolve conflicts. It's also true that there will be personal aspects that you would like to see in your healthy relationships, such as humor or equality.

3. Make a choice

Abuse is a cycle: we say no, and they apologize, although they never really mean it or fake change for a while before the abuse starts again. Only you have the power (and you do have this power within you) to stop the cycle. Make this necessary choice, own it, be proud of it, and above all, stick to it.

4. Be safe

If you fear for your safety in any way, even the slightest bit, you need to find a safe place. It's tough, but staying could result in you or your children ending up in the hospital, and that's never worth staying for. If you don't have a friend or family member you trust, you can reach out to the police and/or local support groups. Try searching for support groups in your area on Facebook.

5. Find your support group

Support comes in many shapes and sizes, even in places you might not imagine. Professional help is a great place to start for emotional healing.

If you aren't comfortable talking to people you know, Facebook groups are an excellent example of people coming together to help each other. Even your neighbors can provide a listening ear and sound advice.

6. Commit to not being a victim

Write a letter of commitment to yourself. I understand that some might feel this is a little corny, but you may be pleasantly surprised by the benefits.

A commitment letter can be a list of "I will not" statements. For example, "I will not let others dictate my life," or "I will not tolerate the silent treatment."

7. Remind yourself that you aren't responsible for the toxic person

We have said enough times that you are not responsible for a toxic person's behavior, but in fact, you aren't responsible for them at all. They are fully functioning adults who also have choices. Don't allow them to manipulate you into staying or doing things because they need you, or they can't survive without you, as this is not a healthy relationship.

8. Process and share your abuse

Some people like physical activities to process their abuse. I find swimming extremely mind-cleansing and makes me feel physically better. Others turn to art, music, or journaling. Sharing your abuse with your support group is a wonderful way to process what you have been through, with nobody judging you.

9. Be kind to your physical self

Your body needs you right now more than ever. Taking care of your body is all part of self-care, and it's often the simple things that will make a big difference, like eating well, drinking plenty of water, and resting when necessary.

Go for a walk and take in nature, meditate, or enjoy a relaxing bath. Take time to do the things you enjoy, whether reading a book or watching a movie. Don't forget to see a doctor about your physical and emotional symptoms.

10. Remember your triggers and boundaries

While we have discussed both at length, these strategies are essential for your recovery. Once you have recognized your triggers and determined your boundaries, remember to check in with them regularly to see if they need updating.

11. Speak up about what you won't tolerate

Another part of breaking the cycle of abuse is to stand up for yourself about the behavior you won't tolerate. Toxic people rely on the fact that you allow them to insult or hurt you so that they feel better. As soon as you put a stop to this, you will notice more balance in the relationship.

12. Understand that it is not your fault

You can admit to making mistakes in the way you have handled toxic people in the past, but that doesn't mean the situation is your fault. It's more than likely that the toxic individuals in your life have a mental disorder—you didn't create this, nor did you encourage it.

13. Let go of guilt and shame

Similarly to the situation not being your fault, there is no reason for you to feel guilt or shame. Processing your traumatic experiences will help you to work through these feelings, enabling you to move on.

14. Find things that make you happy

It has probably been a while since you took the time to do things that make you happy, and you may even have forgotten exactly what that is. Think back to a time in your life before the toxicity. What did you enjoy doing? Are there things that you have always wanted to try? You don't have to spend a lot of money. It could be something as simple as getting in the car and exploring a new area, learning how to cook, or starting a new series.

15. Decide who you can trust

It's normal to be in a stage where you don't trust anyone. While there are abusers and the abused, there are also many other people in the world who are neither. Create two lists—one with the people you can trust and one with those you can't. It won't happen overnight, but gradually, work on allowing yourself to trust these people.

16. Get comfortable with being alone

There is a fine line between spending some quality time alone and social withdrawal. The goal is not to learn how to do everything alone. It's to be comfortable doing everyday things alone before you build up to the bigger things. Time alone increases empathy, productivity, creativity, and mental strength. Enjoy the peace of going for a walk in silence, and work your way up to dining alone. I must say, one of the most empowering experiences in my life was going on vacation alone.

17. Discover ways to build your confidence

Every strategy you try is a step toward a more confident you. Finding your happiness will also start to boost your confidence, but for now, stop comparing yourself to others. Be careful of social media because people rarely post the real version of events, and we end up looking at other people's lives and wishing we were more like them. We never know what's really going on behind each post, so redirect your energy to your own life. Write to-do lists to track the things you are achieving.

18. Give yourself time

They don't call it long-term side effects for no reason. Your commitment and determination are commendable, and you should be proud of this. However, allow time for healing. For some, it could take a couple of months, and for others, it might be years. There is no race! The most important thing is that you are making progress.

19. Keep track of your decision-making skills

This is a great reminder of just how far you have come. You may have noticed that, in the early days, you would question everything, particularly if your abuser was a gaslighter. This would have caused you to doubt your instincts. A lack of sleep and emotional strain also impact your decision-making skills. But, as you start to let go of your emotional abuse, you will realize that your decision-making is more reliable, another way to boost your confidence.

20. Find what works for you

This book is full of advice for not only different types of abuse but also different types of personalities. I know people who have been helped by antidepressants and others who didn't experience any difference; for others, therapy was the solution. You might laugh at the idea of meditation, but the next person can't see how a 4-hour hike helps. We are all individuals and should respect that we will heal in various ways. Give each technique time before disregarding it, and take notes in your journal on the impact of the different strategies you try.

It might be that one technique has a different effect in six months, so it's beneficial to keep track.

Overcoming Anxiety and Depression After Emotional Abuse

People often forget just how complex anxiety and depression are. It's not a simple case of waking up in the morning and changing your mindset. There are techniques like deep breathing and mindfulness that can help relieve the symptoms and allow you the chance to find your strength, but at the same time, it's perfectly normal if you need additional help, and this is where your support system is vital.

When you think of a support system, your mind might jump to friends and family, and while this is a great starting point, it's not always the best for emotional abuse recovery. Our friends and family are some of the most intimate relationships we have, and this can mean that you aren't always comfortable opening up for fear of their reaction. The fear of showing your vulnerabilities to these people can be enough to put you off opening up.

A support system is a network of people who provide an individual with practical or emotional support (Merriam-Webster, n.d.). When you consider this definition, your support system could be made up of a wide range of people, even animals. Research has shown that pet owners are less likely to suffer from depression and have lower blood pressure when dealing with stress (Robinson & Segal, n.d.). That's not to say you should rush out and get a pet if you aren't in the position to take care of one, but spending time with animals can still be a part of your support network if it brings you relief from intense emotions.

When you don't feel comfortable discussing things with people close to you, there are still others who can form part of your support network. There are two main ways to do this: in person and online.

For a more personal approach, you can try joining a group, participating in an activity you like, or starting a new hobby with like-minded people. The same can be said for volunteering for a cause you are passionate about.

There are support groups for anxiety, depression, and emotional abuse, and you can find information about them through local medical professionals. On that note, there is no shame in seeking additional support from medical professionals.

The internet can be an amazing extension of your support network. There are qualified therapists you can find online, whether that's in more formal sessions or even just online. Chatting with a therapist is a way of getting things off your chest, knowing you are in a safe and confidential environment. It's also perfectly understandable if you don't feel like you are in the right place to talk to a professional, but that doesn't mean there aren't other options.

Forums with posts from people who are going through similar experiences can provide comfort. You don't have to share your own experiences. Begin by reading what other people post without any judgment. It might seem they had it worse, but that doesn't invalidate or minimize what you are going through. If you have been controlled, part of your recovery is learning how to take control again, and choosing when you are ready to share is a great start.

Regardless of where you find your support network, it's essential to make an effort to remain in contact with the people in it. I know that life gets busy and time passes without you realizing it, but any type of relationship requires effort from both parties. And fortunately today, there are so many ways to do this.

Send messages, forward memes that make you think of them, or call or video call. You may assume you're being a burden, but try to look at things from a different point of view. Reaching out to them also provides them with the opportunity to expand their own support network.

Moving Forward and Healing Social Connections

Something that people often struggle with after an abusive relationship is reconnecting with old friends and even family members. If a partner has successfully managed to isolate you from others, there could be feelings of guilt and shame for the distance created, as if you blame yourself for the breakdown in the relationship. The first thing to do is change this mindset because it's far from the case. The second thing to do is to reach out to these people because rather than thinking the worst of you, they are probably just generally concerned.

How you reach out is up to you. I know people who have made phone calls and others who have written a letter. The details you go into are also a personal choice. You may want to let them know that you were in an abusive relationship and that you are reconnecting with old friends. You may feel the need to apologize for the lack of contact. Just remember that genuine friendships don't have an expiration date, and although you might need to make an effort to rebuild these bridges, it will be worth it in the end.

There is an elephant in the room that needs addressing, and that is how you rebuild relationships when you are still with an abusive partner. Consider Tania, for example, who had a daughter with her abusive partner, left him once, but then went back. She lost contact with her mom because her mom obviously wasn't happy about her coming back. After getting pregnant again, the relationship with her mom was completely destroyed, and when Tania left for the second time, she was very much alone. It wasn't until after her second child was born and her mom saw that the relationship was definitely over that they were able to start repairing their relationship.

This is something to bear in mind when reconnecting. As much as they will want to be there and support you, they will be concerned about your well-being and your safety. Try to see things from their perspective and understand that they might be dubious if you haven't left the abusive person. It might be that the person has genuinely changed, but they may need time to see these changes for themselves.

On the other hand, it's these people who may be your greatest support if you do decide to leave your abusive partner. This is especially true if you decide to go for the "no contact" approach, as instead of reaching out to contact your ex-partner, you can reach out to these mended relationships.

The "no contact" approach is, as one would imagine, where you have absolutely no contact with your ex-partner, including calls, messages, and engagement in social media such as following or likes. This would also include avoiding social events and possibly social media where you have friends in common. The reason for implementing no contact is that after a breakup, there are bound to be moments when thoughts of the past can stir up emotions. No contact helps you reduce these moments.

If "no contact" is impossible, it's important to reduce the amount of contact as much as possible and perhaps even consider a mediator. Once again, this is where your support system and revived relationships can be helpful.

Navigating New Relationships

There will come a point where a new relationship appeals to you, but there will also be an immense amount of doubt. The first concern will likely be your ability to trust someone after what you have been through. Prior to starting any new relationship, you want to make sure you are in the right position both mentally and emotionally.

It will require time and patience, and during this time, you need to avoid judging yourself for needing this time. When you start to criticize yourself, remind yourself that this is all part of the process. Begin with small and low-stakes situations to start learning how to trust again. This could be opening up to a friend about a secret or asking someone for a favor and trusting them to comply. Reward yourself for each of these steps you take and the gradual process you make. With this ongoing process, you will not only have the necessary time to begin trusting others, but you will also have the time to start trusting yourself and your own instincts. It's your instincts that will enable you to decide when a person is worthy of trusting or not.

When entering new relationships, your boundaries will play a vital role. Know what you want from a relationship and how you want to be treated, and don't be scared to communicate these boundaries in an assertive way early on. The moment something doesn't feel right, the behavior needs to be addressed and consequences clearly explained. You will be stronger this time, so expressing yourself won't be as daunting. Always be aware of the following red flags:

• Name-calling

• Controlling time

• Controlling what you wear

• Gaslighting and questioning your reality

• Jealousy or possessiveness

• Withholding attention or affection

• Requiring you to ask for permission

• Not allowing you to work

• Public embarrassment

• Making you feel guilty when you say no to sex

• Love bombing

As we reach this point, you are now well aware of the red flags to watch out for, as well as your own limitations of what you will tolerate in a relationship. Remain strong and confident in these times, and please don't stay in a new relationship that is potentially abusive for fear of not finding the person you deserve.

Putting Chapter 14 into Practice

Before dating or entering a new relationship, ask yourself the following questions for better clarity:

• Why do you want to start dating?

• What personality traits are you looking for in a partner?

• What are you looking for in the short/long term?

• What worked in your past relationships?

• What are some non-starters that immediately turn you off?

• Are you happy with yourself?

• What are your core values and beliefs?

Exercise: The "Two-Word Mantra"

Choose two words that represent what you want in future relationships (e.g., *calm and respect, honesty and joy*). Repeat them to yourself whenever you start doubting or feeling pulled back into old patterns. This simple mantra will help ground you in what you're aiming for.

Exercise: The "Celebrate One Thing"

Healing is hard work, so each day, celebrate one small thing you did to prioritize yourself. Whether it was declining an invitation you didn't want or taking a walk alone, this exercise is about noticing and celebrating the little wins.

CHAPTER 15: NAVIGATING TOXIC NEGATIVITY

Like drama, some people just thrive on negativity. As we have mentioned, most of us will answer "How are you?" with a good or fine, but we all know at least one person who will start an in-depth discussion about everything negative they can think of. It's draining! However, it's also something we aren't able to completely eliminate from our lives, so it's necessary to learn how to steer through this type of toxic behavior. We will begin by looking inside and questioning our own negativity.

Even the Most Positive People Can't Escape Their Own Negativity

If you're completely honest with yourself, you can admit to having an element of negativity about yourself. That's not to say that you're spreading that negativity among others, but whether it's once in a while or more frequently, negative thoughts creep in.

You might have health problems or financial problems, and of course, we know there are going to be serious issues with your relationships. Any of these can lead us to questions like "Why me?" or "What did I do to deserve this?"

You may start to think about the "if-onlys." *If only I hadn't fallen for that person or taken this job.* After replaying the negativity, you might give yourself a shake and assume that it is what it is and that you have no choice.

If you think about things on a larger scale, life is a string of choices —some are easy, others more challenging, but everything is a choice you get to make. You get to choose what you want for dinner, what time you go to bed, where you go on vacation, and most importantly, the company you keep. From the moment you woke up this morning to now, how many choices have you made? None of them were probably that difficult.

When we listen to our bodies, the choices are actually easy. If you're craving coffee, you need a caffeine boost because your body is tired, so you choose to make a coffee. Logic will also help us to make choices. If you know you need to put gas in the car, you choose to leave earlier for work.

When it comes to our relationships, our emotions can get in the way, making the choices somewhat cloudy, but at the end of the day, the choice is still there. To overcome your own negativity, you need to take responsibility for your actions and accept the fact that nothing will change unless you make a choice. You chose to read this book, which is a giant step in the right direction. The next choice you have to make is what to do with the information.

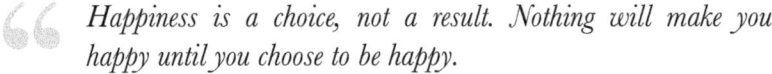 *Happiness is a choice, not a result. Nothing will make you happy until you choose to be happy.*

— *RALPH MARSTON*

Negativity vs. Venting

The question you might be asking now is, "What's the difference between being a negative person and just getting things off your chest?" The answer will always go back to understanding that all emotions are there for a purpose, but how you handle them makes the difference. Anger and frustration can be expressed in a healthy way with a simple "I need to vent. Can I talk to you?"

This way, the other person is not only willing but also prepared. If the moment isn't right, they will more than likely suggest another time. There is no blaming or victimization, nor is there any playing of broken records or multiple topics rolled into one. Venting can feel healthy, like unburdening yourself.

Negativity, on the other hand, is just a case of dumping issues. For the person on the receiving end, it can feel overwhelming or even traumatizing. There is no accountability as the person plays the victim, and any solutions that are offered are dismissed without consideration.

Here are some signs of negativity that can become toxic:

• Constant worrying

• Telling you what to do and how to lead your life

• Negativity is their default mode

• Secrecy is enjoyable

• They expose themselves to too much bad news

• They are overly sensitive, even talking compliments the wrong way

• Being stuck in a comfort zone

• Every sentence ends with the word "but"

• They aren't motivated by achievement

• They miss out on the good things in life

• Good news is spun into a negative

It's important to understand how negativity can quickly turn into full-blown spells of toxicity. If you worry about what others think about you and can calmly express these concerns, you are managing your emotions. If this fear turns you into a people pleaser, your behaviors may become toxic. If you don't learn how to take criticism, you risk becoming defensive.

The point is that the negativity in your life doesn't always come from other people. And, just like our moments of toxic behavior, recognizing this and holding yourself accountable is essential. To do this, you need to understand your triggers.

What Triggers Negativity?

Each of our emotions has triggers. The smell of puppies or freshly cut grass can trigger happiness while watching the news can cause us to feel angry or sad. Negativity can be triggered by some of our most intense emotions. To be able to get ahead of this negativity, you need to analyze what your triggers are. Some common examples include:

• Unfair treatment

• Someone questioning your beliefs or values

• Being ignored, excluded, or rejected

• Feeling emotionally drained by others

• A lack of control or independence

• Betrayal and lies

• Being criticized

• Being disrespected

Of course, negativity can arise from minor issues like traffic to major circumstances such as abusive relationships. Sometimes, our triggers can be from things that have happened in our distant past— parents who were distant can trigger a fear of abandonment.

Learning what your triggers are will lead you to a marvelous place where you are able to make a choice! In the first place, your trigger is there to warn you. You might start to feel negative emotions, or you may have physical symptoms like an increased heart rate, feeling sick, dizzy, or shaking. In between the trigger and your response, you have space. It might only be a split second, but it's still there. At that moment, you have a choice of how you react.

Let's say you have had an incredibly stressful day at work, your body is exhausted, and you are dreading the next day. Your reaction is to have a beer or a glass of wine, but before the negativity overwhelms you, you could choose yoga or meditation instead. If your reaction is to shout at people who frustrate you, you can feel the frustration building up, but before the outburst, you could choose deep breaths to calm yourself and refocus.

After discovering your triggers, it's time to deal with them. There will be some triggers that you can avoid. If you know that a coworker who can't stop complaining goes for a coffee at a certain time, you know not to go at the same time. Nevertheless, this isn't a healthy coping strategy for all of your triggers, as it's impossible to avoid all negativity or never experience negativity.

Space is crucial, and this is not the same as avoiding it. It can be a case of taking a few deep breaths and a mental break from the situation through positive visualization, or it could be excusing yourself for a moment and then returning. This space gives you enough time to manage the physical symptoms the trigger causes and not to react in a negative way—fire won't beat fire. Take this space and use it to pinpoint your emotions without any judgment.

Be aware of projecting negativity. You may find that someone drains you of all your positivity, and you find it all that much harder not to take it out on the next person. It's not fair on others, just like it's not fair to project past experiences onto others either. If you move on from a toxic relationship, though hard, it's not fair to project negativity because you fear the same will happen again.

Finally, watch out for making assumptions and not keeping an open mind. In my own experience, I have often walked away from someone who is so completely negative that spending time with them hurts, but they can't see it. They aren't out to try and make me feel bad; they just lack the same awareness that you now have. Try communicating your own frustrations and lead with a positive example to encourage them to communicate their intense emotions in the same way.

Naturally, this will take time to master, and you must be patient with yourself. Before expecting to control your response, take some time to look at different situations and note your physical and emotional reactions to really understand what triggers you.

How You Can Set Yourself Up for Success

Negativity from within can be controlled. Negativity from others can be avoided to an extent, but the rest will become much easier to handle when you are thriving.

There are two core ways that you can start taking care of yourself so that you can become more successful—whatever that means to you! Let's begin with what you can do for your physical self:

1. Embrace a routine: Routine provides structure and helps to create a more balanced, organized day. A great way to kick start any day is with a morning routine that makes you happy — perhaps a short cardio workout, walking the dog, or some stretching. These can all help to begin the day in a positive way. Having a plan for your day allows you to maintain control.

2. Focus on how you fuel your body: A healthy breakfast is an ideal way to increase your nutrients and energy intake. If you feel yourself reaching for sugary snacks throughout the day, try choosing things that will boost your mood, like berries, nuts, seeds, and even dark chocolate.

3. Choose the right time of the day for your challenging tasks: Some people thrive in the morning and feel a bit sluggish after lunch, while others are the opposite and take a little time to warm up. If you have a bunch of things that you know are stressful, get them out of the way first. Then, plan your day so that the most taxing tasks are scheduled for when you are at your best.

4. Stop multitasking: We are presented with images of multitaskers being able to achieve more, but the truth is that when we don't put all of our focus on one task, it can take longer and mistakes might be made. This doesn't only apply to work. If you are with your children, be with your children. If you are out for dinner, be in the present and not distracted by your phone.

5. Move, laugh, and play: Anyone stuck sitting at a desk should move around for a few minutes every 30 minutes or so. It's also a good idea to take a walk during your lunch break to increase the oxygen in your brain. Never forget the importance of laughing and having fun, even if it's just for a few minutes throughout your day. Choose an app with brain games, watch your favorite YouTube videos, or phone a friend who makes you laugh.

6. Get the right amount of sleep for your body: Whether you need 6 or 9 hours, make sure you go to bed on time so that your body and mind have the chance to rest and recuperate. Avoid caffeine and alcohol at night. As tempted as you may be to take your phone to bed, try and leave it in the other room. You may find yourself on social media, and there is bound to be some negativity online that you don't need before you go to sleep.

When you take care of your physical self, becoming emotionally successful is effortless, which will also be helped by setting boundaries and reinforcing them. Don't try to push your emotions away or ignore them. It's important to feel, recognize, and process your emotions. Journaling is a great way to get all of those feelings out without fearing judgment from others. Writing will allow you to gain objectivity about different situations and look at things from another point of view.

Envisioning Your Personal Power and Creating a Better Life for Yourself

Another great strategy for navigating your way around the negative is to increase the positive in your life. Although neither good nor bad, as we get older, we gain more and more responsibilities, and one way or another, we can lose our sense of identity and what we consider to be our true selves. It's also likely that we pay too much attention to what society thinks we should be, which is the worst way to lose personal power.

Your personal power is the ability to see yourself as an individual who has strengths, weaknesses, and potential. When we stop fighting who we think we should be, we can access our personal power and use this to work toward our goals and the life we want to lead. Begin by reflecting on your current situation by asking yourself why you are doing the things you do and what you get out of it. Evaluate your situation and your relationships so that you can use all of this information to plan for the future.

After years of dealing with toxic people, reminding yourself just how great you are is hard work. But, at the end of the day, you are amazing. You are a good person who is kind, caring, intelligent, and beautiful. You have your faults because we all do. You might feel like losing a couple of pounds, wishing there were fewer wrinkles, and watching the odd series on Netflix instead of doing something more productive, but none of this takes away from the fact that you are a good person. As you get better at establishing your boundaries and removing toxicity from your life, it will be easier to believe this. You will also turn your attention away from building up those who don't deserve your praise and start dedicating it to those who do. This will help you see what a great person you are, and you will find the personal power needed to create your vision.

Your life vision is how you see your life in the future. It's similar to goals but on a larger scale. It includes your goals and dreams, both personally and professionally, as well as a visualization of how you see your relationships developing over time. Imagine your life vision as a compass that you use to orient yourself in the right direction (www.lifehack.org). Without this vision, it's almost like you have handed your compass to others who will use it to control your life.

You might think it's as simple as asking what you want to do with your life, but it's actually a heavy question that doesn't have a quick answer. Much of the answer comes from the work we have already done, so you have a bit of a head start. Your vision will depend on your values and beliefs, which we examined when creating boundaries. You also need a great deal of planning, which we started with reflecting, evaluating, and planning. Let's start with questions to ask about the present, followed by ones about how you envision your future so that you can work on bridging the two.

Questions that look at your present life:

• What things matter to you at the moment? Disregard the expectations and focus on what truly matters to you!

• What do you want to achieve in your career?

• What do you want more of in life? Will this bring you happiness?

• What kind of relationships do you envision for yourself?

• What are you good at?

• What do you want to accomplish in life?

• What skills would you like to improve on?

• Do you have a passion that you would like to develop?

Pick a moment in the future. This could be 5, 10, or 20 years from now.

Questions that look into your future:

• What will you have accomplished?

• What will you be doing? What does a typical day look like?

• Where are you living? What type of home do you have?

• Who are the people around you?

• What do you look like?

• How are your emotions?

If your life vision makes you feel happy and excited about the future, you know you are on to a winner. If not, some of your ideas will need to be tweaked.

The next step is to plan how you are going to get from A to B. You will likely need to develop new skills or make certain choices you had not thought of before. If you imagine yourself in a big house in the country, you might need to adjust your financial situation in order to get there. If you picture a large family around you, it might be time to consider adopting. Rushing into a relationship just to have children will set your life on a different path.

Remember, there are always options and choices. Finally, break down each area of your vision and work out the steps you need to take to get there. Don't forget to recheck your compass as you meet each milestone so that you are confident you are on the right track.

Your Personal Power Needs a Power Phrase

One final tip for boosting your personal power is to create a power phrase. You have probably heard of mantras and affirmations, short phrases that help you remain focused on a goal or encourage the mind to start believing in what you wish to achieve.

For example, "I believe in my visions," "I love myself," and "I am proud of myself." A power phrase is similar, but as the name implies, it allows us to focus on our inner strengths.

A power phrase can be any short phrase, normally just three words that can be repeated any time you need it. It could be before an important meeting or a crucial conversation. It might be when you are feeling stressed or overwhelmed. Your power phrase is a great tool to use in between a trigger and a reaction to help you calm yourself and refocus as it helps you regain control.

To create your own power phrase, you should go back to your goals and visions of how you see yourself at your absolute best. Select three adjectives that relate to this.

The possibilities are endless, but I will give you some of my favorites:

• Beautiful

- Strong

- Powerful

- Independent

- Capable

- Intelligent

- Masterful

- Grateful

- Talented

- Joyful

- Energetic

- Creative

- Funny

- Loyal

- Brave

- Awesome

- Positive

- Confident

In addition to using your power phrase in times of need, you can incorporate it into your daily routine. Repeat your phrase a few times while you shower, prepare lunch, or drive to work.

Accept, Embrace, and Release Negativity

It's here, and it's not going anywhere! You have the choice to dwell on negativity or rise above it. Choosing to be happy and positive doesn't happen overnight, assuming it will lead to disappointment.

Even after practicing the techniques mentioned, you will still have to deal with the negativity of others. It gets easier when we take care of ourselves and practice self-love. However, learning the "accept, embrace, and release" method will help you protect yourself from the negativity that you can't escape.

Accept things for what they are. To do this, you have to determine whether you have control over the situation and whether or not it is your responsibility. Accept that your colleague just loves to look on the pessimistic side. It's not your responsibility to try and fix it, and you have a choice whether to listen or not.

Embracing negativity is about choosing activities that allow you to process it rather than burying it. Some people choose to write things down in a journal or talk to a friend. Meditation and mindfulness are excellent ways to embrace negativity in the right way so that it doesn't eat away at you. You learn how to inhale your life vision and exhale all that is negative.

If you reach a point when your negativity surrounds you, and you can't free yourself, it's important to get the support you need. Talking to a trusted friend can often help you to release some of these pent-up negative emotions. And there is absolutely no shame in talking to a professional if it means you can break free and take that all-important first step toward a brighter future and a stronger, empowered you.

Putting Chapter 15 into Practice

Identifying your triggers may take a little time, as they won't all come to mind at once. You may need to be with certain people or in specific places before they become apparent. Create a document on your phone where you can list your triggers and start working on accepting your emotions and overcoming negativity.

CHAPTER 16: TAKING BACK YOUR LIFE

At this point, I like to think that readers have a much stronger idea of what they are dealing with, the dangers of not dealing with it, and, of course, after some deep introspection, there is an effective plan in place to start eliminating toxic people and behavior. I also recognize that there might still be some nerves, and not all the techniques are fully mastered.

This final chapter is like the last push to the peak of the mountain that will enable you to see the amazing views all around you.

Why Don't People Support My Choices?

There are many answers to this question. It's amazing how many people in the world are incapable of seeing things from another person's point of view.

Your loved one might genuinely try to understand the choices you make, but they can't. It could be that they are just so concerned about you that the worry comes across as a lack of support. They may have a deep-rooted need to be right, so your choices are always going to be wrong.

As we have seen with toxic people, they are unlikely to support the decisions you make because the end result is that they lose control over you.

When people don't support you, even those closest to you who should always have your back, you have to accept this as part of normal life rather than fight it.

It's not your job to impress others or make choices that continuously benefit others. It's a shame, but even those who have known you the longest may never get their heads around you knowing what is best for your own life. And this is okay.

Try to empathize because this is one way for us to rise above people who don't support us. Maybe they are insecure, envious, or scared of the new things that you want to try.

Go ahead and attempt to explain things in a different way to see if this helps them understand, but know when to draw the line and accept it.

What you should do is remember that you have already wasted too much of your time pandering to the needs of the toxic people in your life. There isn't enough time or energy to spend another minute explaining your reasons to people who aren't going to respect them.

 Your life is made of two dates and a dash. Make the most of the dash.

— LINDA ELLIS

What are you going to do with your dash? While you have decided to rid yourself of the toxic behavior, you also need to stop trying to please everyone else and start putting your passions and dreams first.

Doing the things that fill your heart with motivation, joy, and love will help you live a fulfilling life that isn't full of regrets and "what ifs."

It still might be hard to picture just yet, but you can do anything you want to do. There should be nothing holding you back—especially not self-doubt. Pick any inspirational person: Halle Berry once slept in a homeless shelter, J.K. Rowling was a single mom struggling to pay rent, Steve Jobs dropped out of college after one semester and became a millionaire by the age of 23, Ray Charles, Einstein...

I could go on. Each had massive setbacks and carved their own path away from their difficulties. You can do whatever you want with your dash, and you can do it without the support of others, and you certainly don't need them projecting their limitations onto you.

Why You Need to Own Your Own Life

Owning your own life is about focusing on yourself and being grateful for where you are at this point. It's about regaining control and then protecting it so that nobody else can take it away from you in the future.

Furthermore, you get to live your life by your own values, beliefs, and standards, which builds up confidence and the ability to love yourself.

Sometimes, owning your own life begins with accepting responsibility for where you are today and stopping blaming others. Yes, you may have had a rough childhood, but your parents did the best they could with what they had at the time.

Money might be tight, but you can take responsibility for your budget and make changes. You have made mistakes, been with the wrong people, tolerated too much, whatever it may be, own it.

What has happened in the past isn't a sign of what's to come in the future because every day is a new beginning with new opportunities.

Remember how we began by looking at our own negativity. Now is the time to check in with your attitude again and see if those negative thoughts are cropping up every now and again. You may have to keep forcing the positive thoughts until it gets easier to push past negative ideas before you eventually end up unaffected by most negativity.

How to Own Your Own Life

1. Be more intentional with your time and your outlook

While breakfast is the most important meal of the day, your mornings are also the most valuable time. When your morning starts well, the rest of the day tends to follow suit.

Having a morning routine ensures you can start your day with a healthy meal, some exercise, or meditation. It's a precious time for preparation and calm. For mental preparation, you can prepare your to-do list and check your goals.

You can be intentional about maintaining a positive attitude and keeping clear of negative people, even negative news. When you are intentional about the information you share, it is easier to keep negativity out of your life.

2. Become more disciplined

Increasing your self-discipline is more than just a way to achieve your goals by removing distractions and temptations. It's about enhancing your resilience for different situations. When you are more disciplined, you have more control over your life, and this will have a positive effect on your levels of anxiety.

Setting goals is a great way to stay motivated and maintain discipline. Begin by setting small goals that are easy to achieve. Your confidence will build with every small goal you achieve, and you'll soon be tackling the larger ones.

Keep your goals where you can see them. I still prefer pen and paper, but I know others who create digital lists on their phone. Whether it's your to-do list or your goals, make sure you are prioritizing.

For those days when you can't find the motivation, you have to force yourself to get up and take action. There is no room for excuses or feeling sorry for your situation. Count down from ten, visualize yourself achieving your goal, and get moving.

3. Treat yourself like you are a guest

If you have ever had visitors stay, you will know that there is a mad rush of tidying, cleaning, and watering the plants. The best food is prepared, and the finest wine is opened. But why don't we treat ourselves in the same manner?

Even behavior like this shows that we place other people before ourselves. In fact, having a well-organized and clean home is extremely important for your self-care, and a decluttered home helps you develop a decluttered mind. Take some time to declutter your home, and every time you leave the house, leave it as if you were preparing for a guest. Coming home will be all the more rewarding.

4. Try new experiences

Not everyone has a passion for trying new things. It involves stepping out of our comfort zone. We might feel like we are destined to fail, we aren't good enough, or we don't have the skill or knowledge. Such beliefs will only hold us back from a world of so many amazing experiences, and we must get out there and explore the most amazing things in the world.

Again, start with baby steps. Plant some seeds and see what grows, ride a horse, eat new dishes. A famous weightlifting coach had some wise words, "Sorry, you just are not good enough to be disappointed" (Dan John). It sounds harsh, but as we venture into new experiences, there is no justification for our disappointment. If you've been gardening for ten years and your seeds still aren't growing, then it's understandable to be disappointed!

5. Embrace life's lessons

I've recently started growing my first peppers, so I'll stick to my seed analogy! I've tried growing so many things, but nothing ever turned out quite right. I learned that I had planted them in the wrong season, drowned the seeds, left them in the sun and then the rain, and so on. Finally, I got it right.

Wherever you look, life has lessons to teach that you have to embrace. Beforehand, you would have looked at your toxic relationships as a bad thing, and they certainly were. But you have been able to learn so much about yourself and dealing with other people that your life is going to do a complete 180. Keep calm in the face of change, know that you are getting wiser, and keep learning along your path.

6. Create a strategy for your goals

So many people fail to achieve their goals because they haven't planned. It's not enough to say, "I want to be mortgage-free in 15 years" or "I want to take that cruise in two years."

Both of these are significant goals, and writing them down makes them more concrete, but it doesn't automatically mean they are going to happen. Both short- and long-term goals need to be broken down into smaller, achievable steps.

Working on smaller steps is easier to achieve. You start to see progress with the bigger goals, and it helps to keep these bigger goals in sight.

7. Stop waiting for others

Remember when you were in high school, and you and your best friend had your parallel lives all planned out? In an ideal world, our paths would be in sync with our loved ones, but more often than not, you will find yourself waiting for others, preventing you from pursuing the things you want to do. Is it fair that your career advancement gets put on hold so that your partner can fulfill their dreams?

Discussing and agreeing on major life changes is healthy, but constantly waiting for others is unhealthy. To own your own life, you need to set a timeline for your goals and dreams and make this your priority.

8. Build a routine that is enlivening and keeps you centered

A good routine is essential for building healthy habits in your day. When we start practicing healthy habits regularly, stress levels are reduced, anxiety is controlled, and as time management improves, we will have more free time to do the things we enjoy.

Keeping fit has to be a priority if you want to feel good about yourself and stay mentally and physically sound.

Your fitness can include aerobic and muscular fitness as well as flexibility (American College of Sports Medicine). Nutrition, sleep, emotional and mental health will also impact fitness (Oken, 2019).

Here are some ideas you can incorporate into your daily routine:

• Give yourself plenty of time in the morning so that you don't start the day in a rush.

• Eat your fruits and veggies; take vitamin supplements if necessary.

• Make sure your diet is balanced so you are fueling your body with the energy it needs.

• Drink plenty of water; put slices of fruit in the water if it encourages you to drink more and have a glass of water with every other beverage.

• Avoid sugar and caffeine because although it gives us a quick boost of energy, you might find your blood sugar levels remain too high, and this can lead to complications with diabetes or heart disease.

• Increase your heart rate. It's great to start your day with a short cardio session to get the body moving and the oxygen flowing to the brain, followed by a refreshing shower. Start your day at your best.

• Move about during the day. For those who have a desk job, it's important to move regularly. Try taking the stairs instead of the elevator and don't feel guilty for walking away from your desk for a few minutes. The time you are at your desk will be more productive and your eyes get a break from the screen.

• Spend time doing something you love. This could be 20 minutes of reading a book, talking to a friend, scrolling through social media, or one of your hobbies.

• Take five minutes of me-time every day. This isn't the same as hobby time. This is five minutes of nothingness—no technology, no TV—just sit down and watch the world in a peaceful, calm state. Take in all of the positivity around you.

• Set time limits for your activities. Make sure they are realistic, or you will find yourself unable to complete everything, which is not motivating. Being strict with your time will reduce stress and allow you to achieve the most you can.

• Write your to-do list the day before to prevent yourself from worrying about it the next day when you should be relaxing.

• End the day by disconnecting from electronic devices. Instead, write down three positive things about your day.

9. Practice yoga and mediation

Neither yoga nor meditation is as hippy as it may seem. They are valuable tools to assist with both the body and the mind. Certain yoga poses will help you to detect imbalances in the body and increase energy flow.

It's the kind of thing you won't believe until you try, but even after just one session, you'll feel a difference, such as an amazing sense of calm and stretching your body, which is energizing.

I use the app FitOn for guided yoga sessions. And there are also lots of other short workouts that are great for the mornings. Meditation encourages a state where you detach from the emotional situation so that your brain guides you toward a state of tranquility.

Meditation can be used as a rapid response technique for times of stress or depression, but as you don't need very long, you can take just five minutes to meditate throughout the day.

It's not always easy to clear your mind, so I recommend apps like

Headspace to guide you through meditation and help you focus on your breathing.

10. Own your life affirmation

Hopefully, you have created some affirmations for personal empowerment. If you are still playing around with some ideas, you might want to think about affirmations for owning your life:

• I am supposed to be where I am today.

• I am supposed to look the way I do.

• The events in my life have led me to the right place today.

• I am where I am for a reason.

You can be as creative as you want to be and even add some powerful adjectives to the ideas above.

Don't feel overwhelmed by all of these ideas. When you consider all the other tips and techniques we have looked at in this book, you probably feel that there is a lot to do. While this is true, it's always better to start making small changes that will last than to rush everything at once.

Putting Chapter 16 into Practice

Out of all the self-care ideas presented in this chapter, write a list of the ones you believe would be most beneficial. Which item from your list can you start today? Take a calendar or journal and now plan a realistic way to integrate all of the healthy habits you want to adopt.

CONCLUSION

Difficult people are everywhere. It doesn't matter how old you are, what you look like, who you love, or how you make a living—you will meet them. They might hide in plain sight, lure you with kindness, compliments, and love, and then reveal their true colors, but as the old saying goes, it's hard to avoid running into difficult people.

Fighting these toxic souls? Well, that's a losing battle, and you know it. You've spent months—maybe years—trying to mold something complicated into something healthy, only to find yourself drained, emotionally exhausted, or worse. It's not just time wasted; it's pieces of yourself you're trying to reclaim. You've given them the benefit of the doubt, only to watch your generosity evaporate into thin air.

Instead of repeatedly asking, "Why me?" or "What did I do to deserve this?" you've made the empowering choice to reclaim your life. Remember, you haven't done anything wrong. If this person hadn't attached themselves to you, they would have found someone else to mistreat. Now is the moment to transform these painful experiences into valuable lessons and let go of your suffering.

You may still feel fragile in the days and weeks ahead and might not be ready to confront the toxic people in your life. That's okay! The first crucial step is self-reflection and planning. Take the time to evaluate your relationships. Create three columns: one for good relationships, one for those that need work, and one for the people you want to eliminate from your life. Reassess your goals, identify what makes you happy, and envision how you want your life to look in one, five, and ten years. While it's hard to admit our faults, look within to see what changes you can make to foster a more positive outlook.

When it comes to the real heavy-hitters—the sociopaths and master manipulators—you're going to need more than a list. These people are Olympic-level in their ability to twist your emotions and wriggle back into your life. Make sure you're emotionally strong enough to stand your ground. Start with the changes you'd like to see in the difficult people around you, focusing on friends who will understand when you share your feelings. As you see progress, build confidence, and then firmly address those whose toxic behavior has hurt you the most.

Never forget that your safety comes first. If someone has been aggressive toward you in the past or you fear they might harm you physically, don't try to confront them alone. You are not responsible for their reactions but must prioritize your safety.

Practice what you want to say to a difficult person before you speak with them. Use "I" statements instead of "you" to avoid sounding accusatory. Preparation will positively influence how you deliver your message. Remember that any boundaries you set should have consequences you're willing to enforce. Expect pushback and harsh comments from them—this is on them, not you. You have the power to choose how you respond to difficult people and to rise above their negativity.

This is a process, not a sprint. There will be setbacks. Some days you'll feel on top of the world, and there will be days when you'll wonder if you've made any progress at all. But eventually, the bad days will fade. You deserve happiness, respect, and appreciation.

You have the right to live your life as you wish. By removing toxic individuals who refuse to change, you'll make space for healthier relationships, and your newfound wisdom will guide you in nurturing these connections. Don't be too harsh on yourself; you're still allowed to make mistakes. Learn and let go!

And let me leave you with this: just because someone else is determined to live in misery doesn't mean you have to pull up a chair at their pity party. Remember, there's only one dash between your dates—life is too short not to have fun. Smile, laugh, dance, sing, take pride in who you are, and most importantly, be happy!

Now, let's be honest—this isn't a magic solution. If one self-help book could fix everything, we'd all be walking around with perfect skin and halos, casually sipping cold brew in emotional equilibrium. The reality? Life is messy. Relationships are complicated. And toxic people? They're kind of like pigeons—impossible to avoid entirely.

But the good news is, you're not powerless. If you've made it this far, you've already taken a giant step toward reclaiming your life. Whether it's setting boundaries or finally telling that one friend (you know the one) that you don't need their constant passive-aggressive comments about your choices, you're now armed with knowledge, clarity, and—most importantly—perspective.

If you found this book helpful, I'd be forever grateful if you could take a moment to leave a quick review on Amazon. Who knows? Maybe together we can help a few more people navigate the wild and wonderful chaos that is life. Best of luck—you've got this!

EXTRA BONUS 1. SHUT DOWN TOXIC TALK - SMART SCRIPTS FOR STICKY SITUATIONS

I'd like to give you a complimentary cheat sheet to show my appreciation for your purchase!

This cheat sheet includes:

✓ **Powerful Phrases** to shut down negativity without sounding rude

✓ **Smart Responses** for common sticky situations

✓ **Tips on Staying Calm** and keeping your cool

This quick guide is packed with practical advice to help you stay grounded and take charge in any conversation. Don't miss out!

To receive your free cheat sheet, scan the QR code below:

Trouble downloading the checklist? Email me at **chase@chasehillbooks.com**, and I'll send it right over.

Thank you for being here, and happy reading! May these scripts help you find calm, clarity, and maybe even a little fun in the art of conversation.

EXTRA BONUS 2. HOW TO DEAL WITH A TOXIC PERSON: PRACTICAL WORKBOOK

As a special thank you, here's your second complimentary workbook!

This workbook includes:

✓ **Guided Exercises** to identify and address toxic behavior

✓ **Practical Tips** for setting boundaries and protecting your energy

✓ **Guided Reflections** for greater clarity and calm

Ready to take control? This workbook offers step-by-step exercises and proven techniques for managing toxic relationships without losing your sanity.

To receive your free cheat sheet, scan the QR code below:

Trouble downloading the checklist? Email me at **chase@chasehillbooks.com**, and I'll send it right over.

Think of this workbook as your personal toolkit for dealing with toxic personalities. Download it now and start building the boundaries you deserve.

SUMMARY GUIDE

A Short Message from the Author

I hope you're enjoying the book so far! I have a tiny favor to ask that could make a huge difference. If you could take just 30 seconds to leave a review on Amazon, I would be incredibly grateful.

Reviews are super important for authors—they help us get noticed and keep doing what we love. Yet, they're surprisingly hard to come by!

If you've got a moment to spare and some thoughts to share, I'd love to hear what you think. Even a few words would mean the world to me.

Just scan the QR code on the left to leave a review on Amazon

Chapter 1: Difficulty: The Only Consistency

The human brain is an incredible yet complex organ with billions of connections and continuous messaging. Neurochemicals and personality types significantly impact our behavior, and in some cases, they contribute to the development of personality disorders. Parenting styles also play a role, but it's safe to say that toxic behaviors are a combination of both nature and nurture. If someone has experienced trauma in childhood or other past events, it can affect how they treat others. This means that although these behaviors are inexcusable, they aren't always intentional. Change may not come from the toxic people in your life, but it has to come from you if you want to experience a difference.

• Toxicity exists on a spectrum, from energy vampires to physically and emotionally abusive people.

• Chemical imbalances, particularly serotonin deficiencies, can affect emotions and mental health, leading to impulsive, aggressive behavior.

• People aren't born toxic; understanding a person's past can help you understand their current behavior.

• Overcoming toxicity isn't about fixing another person. It's about healing and personal growth for your own physical and emotional well-being, and even for your safety.

Chapter 2: Sometimes We're the Problem

Nobody is perfect, and although it can be difficult to accept our faults, there is a big difference between having a toxic moment (like snapping after a hard day) and being toxic (constant snapping, often without a valid reason). Behavior is subjective, and we don't always share the same opinions on what constitutes toxicity. One person might be deeply offended by a sexist joke, while another may not be affected. Self-awareness and acceptance are crucial for taking responsibility for your own behavior.

• Toxicity is defined as any behavior that causes harm to others. Even good people can have toxic moments.

• Part of the healing process is recognizing your own toxic behaviors and addressing them, holding yourself accountable.

• Turn negative experiences into learning opportunities rather than letting them fester and become toxic.

• Be mindful of the victim complex, whether it's coming from you or someone else using it to manipulate you.

Chapter 3: Change Starts with You

You may feel like all your power has been stripped away, but now is the time to take it back. Routines, self-care, and spending time with people who make you feel positive are the foundations of your empowerment. You have choices, and one of those choices is to break free from limiting beliefs you have about yourself.

• Regularly remind yourself of your positive qualities to rediscover your strength.

• Speak the truth about your situation, even if it's just to one trusted friend, so you aren't suffering in silence.

• You don't need to change yourself to please others. Make changes to please yourself.

• Take time to determine what behaviors you will tolerate and what you won't. Understand what is within your control and what is not.

Chapter 4: Sociopathy 101: Understanding Sociopaths

A sociopath is someone who has no regard for other people's feelings and does not behave in ways that are socially acceptable. They lack empathy and rely on manipulation. Sociopaths show no guilt for the pain they cause. Although sociopaths share similarities with psychopaths, psychopaths can pretend to care. It's believed that sociopathic behavior is created, whereas psychopathy is inborn.

• Sociopaths are charming; they can seem trustworthy, but they will use your vulnerabilities as ammunition.

• They don't play by the rules and have no problem lying or being disloyal.

• Everything will be your fault, and you will be blamed for all the problems in their life.

• A sociopath's personality runs hot and cold, making it difficult to know what to expect.

Chapter 5: Fighting the Sociopath

One of the hardest decisions you may face is whether to stay with a sociopath or not, and only you can make that choice. If you decide to stay, it's crucial that you prioritize your safety. Trust your instincts, but always have a plan to leave if you feel in danger. Understanding the stages of trauma bonding can help you recognize and stop certain behaviors.

• Only share what is absolutely necessary, and avoid being the subject of conversations.

• Set boundaries, communicate them, and stick to them.

• Pay attention to the positive changes they make, not the promises they say they'll make.

• Take time to process your emotions. Acknowledge and accept them as part of your healing journey.

Chapter 6: Narcissism 101: Understanding Narcissists

All sociopaths have narcissistic traits, but not all narcissists are sociopaths. There are many misconceptions about narcissism, and this confusion is compounded by the overuse of the term. While narcissism isn't uncommon, narcissistic personality disorder is. Though there are different types of narcissism—one of them even being healthy—narcissists generally see themselves as more important than others. They may appear extremely confident, lack empathy, and constantly seek admiration or perfection.

• Despite their outward appearance, narcissists often have incredibly low self-esteem. They are insecure and envious of the attention others receive.

• They need to be in control, and your attempts to break free from that control can cause them to become angry or revert to manipulation.

• Gaslighting is a common technique used by narcissists, causing you to doubt everything, even your own reality.

• Apologies are unlikely because they believe they have done nothing wrong.

Chapter 7: Overcoming the Narcissist

Overcoming narcissistic behavior requires 100 percent commitment from you. If you start thinking they will change, you may lose the determination to make the necessary changes in your own life. An important step forward is for the narcissist to recognize that they need professional help. Whether or not they get help, boundaries are essential. To establish and maintain them, you need to prioritize your mental and emotional well-being through self-care.

• Surround yourself with strong, positive people. Don't allow the narcissist to isolate you from your support system.

• Don't get sucked into their emotional games. Remember that they will use your reactions against you.

• If you choose to leave a narcissist, avoid the breakup-makeup pattern, as it will only prolong your suffering. Make a clean break whenever possible.

• Give yourself time to heal from the trauma stored in your body before starting a new relationship. Know what you want from your life to avoid entering future relationships with narcissists.

Chapter 8: Sometimes It's Neither

People with borderline personality disorder, bipolar disorder, and other mental or personality disorders can sometimes exhibit toxic behaviors. Whether you choose to tolerate their behavior may depend on their willingness to get help. However, not all toxic behavior is obvious. Excessive sarcasm, over-competitiveness, and the need to fix everyone are examples of subtle toxic behaviors that we can all be guilty of.

• Everyone is capable of toxic behavior, but a toxic person won't recognize their actions or make amends.

• Beware of love causing blindness to toxicity. Jealousy is not a sign that someone loves you.

• Toxic behaviors can vary depending on the type of relationship. Your family may try to control your life, while your friends may not respect your boundaries on social media.

• Change is possible, but that doesn't mean you need to give toxic people unlimited chances to right their wrongs.

Chapter 9: The Real Problem: Manipulation

Manipulation is the act of controlling someone for your own advantage. It's incredibly toxic because it discourages people from trusting their instincts and often leads them to do things they don't want to do. This can leave a person feeling drained as they constantly try to please others, and it can also lead to anxiety and depression. Manipulation can be conscious or unconscious, but it is often subtle.

• The Dark Triad consists of narcissism (a superior sense of self and lack of empathy), psychopathy (charming but selfish), and Machiavellianism (using manipulation).

• Manipulative behaviors include lying, passive aggression, gaslighting, using sex as a tool, and the silent treatment.

• These behaviors often start small, like saying they prefer you in a particular outfit, but can end up controlling more areas of your life.

• Be aware of phrases like "You're being dramatic" and "You're imagining things" because you probably aren't.

Chapter 10: Beating Manipulation

To overcome manipulation, you need to recognize it and put a stop to it in order to regain control. Many examples of manipulation are hard to spot, such as when someone does something intentionally to hurt you but then plays dumb. It's essential to listen to and trust your instincts. Know that you have the right to say no—and mean it!

• All human beings are free and equal. Don't let anyone make you feel otherwise.

• Prioritizing your needs doesn't make you selfish. Don't blame yourself if others can't understand this.

• Try turning the focus back on the manipulator to highlight their behavior instead of tolerating it.

• "No" is a complete sentence and doesn't need to come with an apology.

Chapter 11: Communication ≠ Powerlessness

Communicating with a toxic person can be a turning point. It can open doors, provide a chance to be vulnerable, and create deeper connections. On the other hand, if the relationship isn't progressing, communication can allow for closure or, at the very least, a chance to get things off your chest. Successful communication requires both speaking and listening, as well as a thick skin to handle potential insults.

• Be careful how much emotion you show. If you know the person will use your emotions against you, stay composed.

• Be intentional about your conversation. Stick to the topic, and remember you aren't out to win.

• Know when to use "I" statements to take responsibility for your emotions and "We" statements to create unity.

• Avoid judging the other person. Let them finish speaking before you formulate a response. It's okay to disagree, but ask for their opinions as well.

Chapter 12: Dealing with Difficult People

It's not just romantic relationships that can be toxic. Unfortunately, difficult people can be found in all areas of our lives. Effective communication skills can improve these relationships, but you may need to add a bit more assertiveness, especially when dealing with conflict.

• In addition to manipulators, narcissists, and toxic individuals, difficult people can include drama queens, gossipers, and pessimists.

• Avoiding conflict is unhealthy and may only escalate the problem.

• Perspective is key in conflict resolution. Get good at seeing things from another person's point of view, even if you don't agree with it.

• The sandwich technique (sandwiching a negative between two positives) can be effective in a wide range of relationships and situations.

Chapter 13: Emotional Abuse: Your Guide

Misconceptions about emotional abuse can be extremely dangerous. Assuming it only affects women invalidates men's experiences, and while there are no physical scars, emotional abuse can be just as painful as physical abuse. The consequences of emotional abuse can range from low self-esteem to anxiety and depression. Some people may also experience insomnia or panic attacks, which can impact physical well-being.

• There is no excuse for emotional abuse, but gaining perspective can help you better understand your own experiences and why you are being treated the way you are.

• Reactive abuse is when an abused person becomes the abuser. While it may not be entirely their fault, the abuse is still unacceptable.

• You did not allow this emotional abuse to happen, nor did you do anything to deserve it!

• Reach out for professional help if you are suffering from depression, believe you are suffering, or have any other concerns about your health.

Chapter 14: Healing From Emotional Abuse

To heal, you must first acknowledge your emotional abuse. Take time to consider your physical and mental health and how someone's behavior is affecting you. Because of the long-term effects of emotional abuse, you will need time and patience with yourself. There will come a time when you feel the weight lift off your shoulders, and you'll be ready to move forward with new connections and positive relationships.

• You have the power to stop the cycle of abuse!

• Find your support system, whether it's trusted friends, family, or online resources. Lean on them—they want to help.

• Whenever possible, go for a no-contact approach to reduce painful emotions that arise when ending relationships.

• Know exactly what you won't tolerate, and have these boundaries clear before entering a new romantic relationship.

Chapter 15: Navigating Toxic Negativity

We all need to vent now and again, but venting has a topic, a purpose, and involves asking permission before unloading. Toxic negativity is just complaining for the sake of complaining, and it's draining. Some people love negativity, but you may also find yourself triggered by negative moments such as unfair treatment or being lied to. While you shouldn't force positivity, you can choose to develop a more positive mindset.

• Watch out for energy vampires, such as those who constantly worry, love secrecy, or overuse the word "but."

• Understand your own triggers, and use space to prevent yourself from reacting the wrong way.

• Reflect on your own life to understand what's happening and what you want for the future—not just in your relationships.

• Create your personal power phrase and use it as part of accepting and releasing negativity.

Chapter 16: Taking Your Life Back

You may feel like you've wasted a good portion of your life putting up with toxic people, but it's far from over. Going forward, you can take control and live authentically according to your own values and beliefs. Everything that has happened in your life is an opportunity to learn and protect yourself in the future.

• Set goals for increased motivation, better time management, and greater discipline so you can achieve everything you set out to do.

• Start a new routine for healthy habits that allow for self-care. Begin with the core aspects: sleep, nutrition, and exercise.

• Break out of your comfort zone and try new things. Take time to do the things that make you happy.

• Don't let anyone hold you back, waste your precious time, or stop you from fulfilling your dreams. Own your destiny!

CONTINUE YOUR JOURNEY WITH 'THE ART OF SELF-IMPROVEMENT' SERIES BY CHASE HILL

How to Stop Negative Thinking

This guide breaks down **seven easy steps to tackle everything from fleeting intrusive thoughts to deep-seated ruminations.** With practical strategies, exercises, and tools, it helps you pinpoint the roots of your negative thoughts and offers proven techniques to calm your mind.

Learn how to **shed toxic behaviors and embrace self-love** and acceptance through positive affirmations and self-talk.
If you're ready for a happier, more positive outlook, this guide is your starting point.

Healthy Boundaries

Discover the power of self-love, and learn how to **set healthy boundaries – without feeling guilty**. You don't have to compromise your individuality just to be "considerate" of others. You can set healthy boundaries, and make your friends, family and parents **respect that boundary.**

Setting up boundaries isn't about being rude: it's about acknowledging that **your well-being comes first.** You can start doing what YOU want to do.

Switch Off Overthinking

The modern world fans the flames with its non-stop influx of information, choices to be made, and the pressure to always be switched 'on'. It's no wonder your mind is in overdrive.

But imagine a toolkit, one that's been tested in the trenches of the busiest of minds, offering **not just quick fixes, but sustainable strategies**.

With over 30 strategies to choose from and apply, you can create your own path toward mental peace, emotional resilience, and serenity.

READY FOR MORE INSIGHTS AND INSPIRATION? SCAN THE QR CODE TO FIND MORE BOOKS BY CHASE HILL AND CONTINUE YOUR JOURNEY.

RESOURCES

11 Warning Signs you are Dealing with a Workplace Sociopath. (2022, August 16). *www.marie-claireross.com*. https://www.marie-claireross.com/blog/11-warning-signs-you-are-dealing-with-a-workplace-sociopath

A study of the etiology of sociopathic behavior. (1974a, September 1). PubMed. https://pubmed.ncbi.nlm.nih.gov/17894069/

Alegria, A. A. (2013, July). Sex differences in antisocial personality disorder: results from the National Epidemiological Survey on Alcohol and Related Conditions. PubMed. https://pubmed.ncbi.nlm.nih.gov/23544428/

Altomara, D. (2023, December 26). *Sociopaths: warning signs and red flags.* WebMD. https://www.webmd.com/mental-health/signs-sociopath

American Museum of Natural History. (n.d.). Your Emotional Brain | AMNH. Retrieved July 5, 2021, from https://www.amnh.org/exhibitions/brain-the-inside-story/your-emotional-brain

American Psychiatric Association. (n.d.). What Are Sleep Disorders? Web Starter Kit. Retrieved July 2, 2021, from https://www.psychiatry.org/patients-families/sleep-disorders/what-are-sleep-disorders

Antisocial personality disorder - Symptoms and causes. (n.d.). Mayo Clinic. https://www.mayoclinic.org/diseases-conditions/antisocial-personality-disorder/symptoms-causes/syc-20353928

A-Z Quotes. (n.d.). *Denzel Washington Quote.* https://www.azquotes.com/quote/1281937

Azam, S. (2019, December 19). Brain Chemicals. Peak. https://blog.peak.net/2019/10/29/brain-chemicals/

Barberio, I. (n.d.). *Removing toxicity and letting go of self-limiting beliefs.* Inez Barberio - Emotional Intelligence and Diversity Inclusion. https://www.inezbarberio.com/blog/removing-toxicity-self-limiting-beliefs

Barkley, S. (2023, May 5). *Am I The Problem? 6 Signs of a Person with Toxic Traits.* Psych Central. https://psychcentral.com/relationships/maybe-the-problem-is-you

BetterHelp Editorial Team. (2024, June 4). *Dating a Sociopathic Person: What to be aware of | BetterHelp.* https://www.betterhelp.com/advice/sociopathy/dating-a-sociopath-what-to-be-aware-of/

Bold, S. (n.d.). Emotional Healing with Meditation & Mindfulness | | Healing Holidays. HealingHolidays. Retrieved July 5, 2021, from https://www.healingholidays.com/blog/emotional-healing-with-meditation-mindfulness

Brainy Quote. (n.d.). *Conflict quotes.* https://www.brainyquote.com/topics/conflict-quotes

Brooke, A. (2018, November 7). 4 Ways to Identify Your Own Toxic Behaviors in Relationships. The Temper. https://www.thetemper.com/4-ways-to-identify-your-own-toxic-behaviors-in-relationships/

Charuk, J. (2018, October 18). 6 Steps to Get Rid of Your Limiting Beliefs. Charuk

Studios. http://www.charukstudios.com/blog/6-steps-to-get-rid-of-your-limiting-beliefs

Choi, C. L. Q. (2016, June 20). "Artificial Synapses" Could Let Supercomputers Mimic the Human Brain. Scientific American. https://www.scientificamerican.com/article/artificial-synapses-could-let-supercomputers-mimic-the-human-brain/

Choose to Be Happy with These Happiness is a Choice Quotes. (n.d.). EnkiQuotes. Retrieved June 22, 2021, from https://www.enkiquotes.com/happiness-is-a-choice-quotes.html

Cikanavicius, D. (2018, October 14). *Dangerous dark traits among narcissists, abusers, and toxic people.* Psych Central. https://psychcentral.com/blog/psychology-self/2018/10/dark-narcissist-traits#1

Clear, J. (2019, February 19). You're Not Good Enough to Feel Disappointed. James Clear. https://jamesclear.com/good-disappointed

Cleveland Clinic. (2024, May 1). *Personality disorders.* https://my.clevelandclinic.org/health/diseases/9636-personality-disorders-overview

Collins. (n.d.). *Definition of "victim."* Collins Dictionary. https://www.collinsdictionary.com/dictionary/english/victim

Darcy, A. M., & Jacobson, S. (2023, March 6). *Traumatic Bonding – How to break free of trauma bonds.* Harley Therapy™ Blog. https://www.harleytherapy.co.uk/counselling/traumatic-bonding-break-trauma-bonds.htm

Dark Triad. (n.d.). Psychology Today. https://www.psychologytoday.com/us/basics/dark-triad

Dawn. (2021, January 29). *"Respond intelligently even to unintelligent treatment."* One Smart Fortunate Cookie. https://onesmartfortunatecookie.wordpress.com/2019/06/02/respond-intelligently-even-to-unintelligent-treatment/

Day, C. (2020, June 19). *I worked for a sociopath and here's what it's like. . .* https://www.linkedin.com/pulse/i-worked-sociopath-heres-what-its-like-christine-day/

Dialogues Clin Neurosci. (2010, March 1). The genetic epidemiology of personality disorders. PubMed Central (PMC). https://www.ncbi.nlm.nih.gov/pmc/articles/PMC3181941/

Doll, B. R. (2012, November 7). How to Recognize a Sociopath. Agnesian HealthCare. https://www.agnesian.com/blog/how-recognize-sociopath

Dombeck, M., PhD. (n.d.). Nature, Nurture and Psychopathy—Personality Disorders. Mental Health. Retrieved July 5, 2021, from https://www.mentalhelp.net/blogs/nature-nurture-and-psychopathy/

Dr. Ramani. (2020, July 13). 11 tactics for not letting narcissists into your life in the first place [Video]. YouTube. https://www.youtube.com/watch?v=UdcGsbcANj8

Evenson, R. (2013). Powerful Phrases for Dealing with Difficult People: Over 325 Ready-to-Use Words and Phrases for Working with Challenging Personalities (1st ed.). AMACOM Books.

Friedman, W. J. (n.d.). Developing An Inner Meter on Manipulation—A Critical Life Skill—Wellness, Disease Prevention, And Stress Reduction Information. Mentalhelp.Net. Retrieved June 21, 2021, from https://www.mentalhelp.net/blogs/developing-an-inner-meter-on-manipulation-a-critical-life-skill/

Habits: How They Form and How To Break Them. (2012, March 5). Npr.Org.

https://choice.npr.org/index.html?origin=https://www.n-pr.org/2012/03/05/147192599/habits-how-they-form-and-how-to-break-them?t=1625241026390

Health Benefits of Social Interaction—Mercy Medical Center. (n.d.). Mercy Care. Retrieved July 5, 2021, from https://www.mercycare.org/bhs/eap/resources/health-benefits-of-social-interaction/

How to Heal from Emotional Abuse: The Ultimate Guide to Recovery [Update 2023]. (2023, July 5). Eddins Counseling Group – Houston & Sugar Land, TX. https://eddinscounseling.com/how-to-heal-from-emotional-abuse/

Ifeanyi, D. (2022, August 22). Are you a people pleaser? [+ How to stop being too Nice in 3 simple steps]. *Pawns: Grow up - Level up - Step Up.* https://pawns.com.ng/people-pleaser/

Itani, O. (2021, February 28). You Are What You Think: How Your Thoughts Create Your Reality. OMAR ITANI. https://www.omaritani.com/blog/what-you-think

Janecic, P. (2020, June 1). How Your Perception Creates a Different Reality. Mind of Steel. https://themindofsteel.com/perception/

Journal of Women's Health. (2011, December). Sleep Disturbances and Their Association With Mental Health Among Women Exposed to Intimate Partner Violence. Www.Ncbi.Nlm.Nih.Gov. https://www.ncbi.nlm.nih.gov/pmc/articles/PMC3236986/

Katherine, C.-A. (2022, February 8). Healing Doesn't mean the damage never existed. *The Graceful Boon - A Guide To Women's Issues.* https://thegracefulboon.com/2022/02/08/healing-doesnt-mean-the-damage-never-existed/

Kass, A. (n.d.). How To Heal From Emotional Abuse [7-steps]. Go Smart Life. Retrieved July 5, 2021, from https://www.gosmartlife.com/emotional-abuse-in-marriage/emotional-abuse-healing

Khoddam, R. (2014, August 20). The Truth Will Set You Free. Psychology Today. https://www.psychologytoday.com/us/blog/the-addiction-connection/201408/the-truth-will-set-you-free

Kryger, K. (2023, December 24). *105 Toxic People Quotes to help get rid of the negativity in your life.* Parade. https://parade.com/living/toxic-people-quotes

Lancer, D. (2018, December 10). Beware of the Malevolent Dark Triad. Psychologytoday. https://www.psychologytoday.com/us/blog/toxic-relationships/201812/beware-the-malevolent-dark-triad

Lancer, D. (2023, August 1). *Myths about narcissism.* What Is Codependency? https://whatiscodependency.com/myths-about-narcissism/

Letting it go: getting past negative emotions. (n.d.). https://www.columbiadoctors.org/health-library/article/letting-it-go-getting-past-negative-emotions/

The link between serial killers and head trauma. (n.d.). Crime+Investigation UK. Retrieved July 2, 2021, from https://www.crimeandinvestigation.co.uk/article/the-link-between-serial-killers-and-head-trauma

Live Your Dream—Life, Business, Career & Health Coaching. (2019, November 28). Move Beyond | Live Your Dream. http://www.movebeyond.net

Lpcc, S. S. (2019, October 11). *Coping with Sociopaths (Antisocial Personality Disorder).* Psych Central. https://psychcentral.com/pro/recovery-expert/2019/10/coping-with-sociopaths-antisocial-personality-disorder#1

McAvoy, K., PhD. (2020, September 24). How to Survive Living with a Sociopath - Kerry McAvoy, PhD. *Kerry McAvoy*. https://kerrymcavoyphd.com/how-to-survive-living-with-a-sociopath/

Manipulation. (2019, March 26). GoodTherapy.Org Therapy Blog. https://www.goodtherapy.org/blog/psychpedia/manipulation

Main, N. (2024, March 18). The sociopath next door: Middle-class LA mom-of-two reveals what it's REALLY like living with. . . *Mail Online*. https://www.dailymail.co.uk/sciencetech/article-13196853/Sociopath-battling-personality-disorder.html

Marripedia. (n.d.). Effects of Divorce on Children's Future Relationships [Marripedia]. Www.Marripedia.Org. Retrieved July 2, 2021, from http://marripedia.org/effect_of_divorce_on_children_s_future_relationships

Martens, W. H. J., MD PhD. (2020, July 9). What Lies Behind: The Hidden Suffering of the Psychopath. Psychiatric Times. https://www.psychiatrictimes.com/view/what-lays-behind-the-hidden-suffering-of-the-psychopath

Matsumoto, D. (2019, December 4). The Seven Basic Emotions: Do You Know Them? David Matsumoto. Medium. https://davidmatsumoto.medium.com/the-seven-basic-emotions-do-you-know-them-66e6564b0208

Mayo Clinic. (n.d.). Narcissistic personality disorder—Symptoms and causes. Retrieved July 5, 2021, from https://www.mayoclinic.org/diseases-conditions/narcissistic-personality-disorder/symptoms-causes/syc-20366662

McGregor, J. (2014, December 2). Breaking Up With A Sociopath. Welldoing. https://welldoing.org/article/breaking-up-with-a-sociopath

Merriam-Webster. (n.d.). Support system. In *Merriam-Webster Dictionary*. https://www.merriam-webster.com/dictionary/support%20system

mindbodygreen. (2021, June 30). There Are At Least 8 Types Of Narcissists—Which Ones Are Dangerous?https://www.mindbodygreen.com/articles/types-of-narcissists

MindTools | Home. (n.d.). https://www.mindtools.com/axtfdfb/dealing-with-manipulative-people

Morin, A. (2017, August 7). 7 Science-Backed Reasons You Should Spend More Time Alone. Forbes. https://www.forbes.com/sites/amymorin/2017/08/05/7-science-backed-reasons-you-should-spend-more-time-alone/?sh=75a9bc711b7e

NNEDV. (2016, November 3). *Emotional abuse is anything but "Tender": Myths and reality.* https://nnedv.org/latest_update/emotional-abuse-anything-tender-myths-reality/

Pietrangelo, A. (2019, March 6). 10 Tips for Dealing with a Narcissistic Personality. Healthline. https://www.healthline.com/health/how-to-deal-with-a-narcissist

Psychology Today. (n.d.). *Trauma bonding*. https://www.psychologytoday.com/us/basics/trauma-bonding

The Power of Acceptance | Dylan Woon | TEDxKangar. (2018, March 30). [Video]. YouTube. https://www.youtube.com/watch?v=-mQKf3Fz5KA

Quoter, H. (2021, March 29). *Just Remember, We are All Toxic*. Fractal Enlightenment. https://fractalenlightenment.com/51182/quotes/just-remember-we-are-all-toxic

Quotes about people talking about you - DesiQuotes.com. (n.d.). https://www.desiquotes.com/quotes-about-people-talking-about-you/

Reader, L. (2023, April 16). *A classic Lovefraud story: I married a sociopath*. Lovefraud |

Escape Sociopaths - Narcissists in Relationships. https://lovefraud.com/a-classic-lovefraud-story-i-married-a-sociopath/

Rebeca Zung. (2020, March 4). Phrases to Disarm a Narcissist [Video]. YouTube. https://www.youtube.com/watch?v=e6vJoq-6mXU

Rhein, W. (2022, November 3). The manipulative way narcissists turn friends & family against you. *Medium.* https://medium.com/heart-affairs/the-manipulative-way-narcissists-turn-friends-family-against-you-147e25149d61

Robinson, L., & Segal, J., PhD. (2024, February 5). The Health and Mood-Boosting Benefits of Pets - HelpGuide.org. *HelpGuide.org.* https://www.helpguide.org/wellness/pets/mood-boosting-power-of-dogs

Sapolsky, R. M. (2020, December 30). The teenage brain: Why some years are (a lot) crazier than others. Big Think. https://bigthink.com/videos/what-age-is-brain-fully-developed

Science Direct. (2014, May 1). Neurodevelopmental and psychosocial risk factors in serial killers and mass murderers. https://www.sciencedirect.com/science/article/pii/S1359178914000305

Shortsleeve, C. (2018, October 16). How to Tell If Someone Is Manipulating You— And What to Do About It. Time. https://time.com/5411624/how-to-tell-if-being-manipulated/

Sterner, S. (2018, January 30). 5 Questions to Help You Stop Being Manipulated. Steph Sterner. https://stephsterner.com/5-questions-help-being-manipulated/

Stillman, J. (2021, January 7). 10 Techniques Used by Manipulators (and How to Fight Them). Inc.Com. https://www.inc.com/jessica-stillman/10-popular-techniques-used-by-manipulators-and-how-to-fight-them.html

Terng, L. Y. (2020, June 6). 5 Things Toxic People Have In Common—Age of Awareness. Medium. https://medium.com/age-of-awareness/5-things-toxic-people-have-in-common-2d50a8723e7c

Tolles, J. (2017, January 9). How to Embrace True Power. Spiritual Awakening Process. https://www.spiritualawakeningprocess.com/2017/01/how-to-embrace-true-power.html

Tull, M. (2020, March 22). Coping With Isolation When You Are Suicidal and Have PTSD. Verywell Mind. https://www.verywellmind.com/ptsd-and-suicide-2797540

Types of Depression. (2008, May 22). WebMD. https://www.webmd.com/depression/guide/depression-types

Universidad Carlos III de Madrid. (n.d.). A study on human behavior has identified four basic personality types | UC3M. Www.Uc3m.Es. Retrieved July 2, 2021, from https://www.uc3m.es/ss/Satellite/UC3MInstitucional/en/Detalle/Comunicacion_C/1371223155576/1371216052182/A_study_on_human_behavior_has_identified_four_basic_personality_types

Wikipedia contributors. (2021, July 1). Narcissism. Wikipedia. https://en.wikipedia.org/wiki/Narcissism

Young, K. (2021, May 23). Toxic People: 12 Things They Do and How to Deal with Them. Hey Sigmund. https://www.heysigmund.com/toxic-people/

Zobolas, C. (2024, July 8). *Forming Healthy Relationships After Abuse | Denver, CO — Chadley Zobolas Therapy Group.* Chadley Zobolas Therapy Group. https://www.chadleyzobolastherapy.com/blog/forming-healthy-relationships-after-abuse

www.ingramcontent.com/pod-product-compliance
Ingram Content Group UK Ltd.
Pitfield, Milton Keynes, MK11 3LW, UK
UKHW011404030625
6213UKWH00024B/373